Not Alone

*From Chasing Connection
To Being Connected*
Belonging and the Power
of Staying

Nancy Deckant

Published by Nashville Cool, LLC

Not Alone
From Chasing Connection to Being Connected:
Belonging and the Power of Staying

Print ISBN: 979-8-9955324-0-8
eBook ISBN: 979-8-9955324-1-5

First Edition

Order Information: nancydeckant.com
For Permission contact: nancy@nashvillecool.com
https://www.nancydeckant.com

Published by Nashville Cool, LLC
© 2026 Nancy Deckant
Printed in the United States of America

Cover Art & Design: Nancy Deckant
Photography: Joe Scot Schroeder

Disclaimer: This book and its associated website are intended for informational and reflective purposes only and do not constitute medical, psychological, or therapeutic advice. The author and publisher are not licensed therapists, psychologists, or counselors. Readers seeking mental health support should consult a qualified professional.

Table of Contents

This book waited patiently for me until I was ready to listen.

Writing it gave tender experiences a place to stand, allowing the quiet language of the body to become something I could recognize and feel less alone inside—

as if these pages were keeping me company

while I learned how to keep myself company.

At the Threshold

If you carry pain in your body—if you have listened, tried, stayed
with the ache, maybe seen a counselor—You're not alone, honey!

Truth is—something in you has been trying to speak for a long time.

You may know what happened to you to cause the pain. You may
not. You may have stories of trauma. Some of them healed enough
that they no longer hurt the way they once did.

And still, something lingered—Not loud. Not dramatic.
Just… somehow unresolved.

You learned how to listen inside.
You noticed that thoughts often began as sensations—

a tightening,
an ache in your mid-section,
a heaviness,
a quiet pull,
a loud, unyielding pull—

and that if you stayed with the feeling,
you could almost hear it speak.

This is what I discovered:
that was only the top layer.

Pain is not a single truth.
It's an iceberg.

At the surface, it warns:
stay away—you're going to wreck.
Or it beckons:
come closer—there's something deeper to explore.

And the only way through is listening.
Again. And again. Every day, if necessary.

That kind of listening requires staying.
Not leaving it by itself.
Not rushing it to make sense.

Staying until the tears come.
Staying until the ache gives way.
Staying until what lives underneath—

The truth about you,
The truth of how you felt becomes unmistakable.
Until that truth finally finds a home in your body.

Until it settles as peace.

Keep listening—

I used to understand life from my head and heart,
a real brainiac living on smarts and intuition.

Now I feel life from the inside out.
I have access to all of me.
My body weighs in on what happens to me.

I belong to myself. That's what's different.

I didn't learn my way into this.
I simply stopped leaving myself.

And when I stayed, something inside me began to trust me again.
And when *that* happened, something surprising followed.

The connection I had spent a lifetime chasing was suddenly
already here. Closer than I ever imagined.

I'm with me.
I'm in me.
I'm smiling.
I belong—to me.

No one could ever take this.

There isn't a chance on this planet
that I would ever be split from myself again.

And the wonder is:

Belonging has structure.
And staying—
staying with yourself,
staying with your body,
staying in the truth of the moment
builds it.

It's a moon landing.

I will never be the same.
The whole world will always
be different because of it.

And I'm not here to explain it—

I'm here for you to witness it.

1. The Loneliness That Looked Like Independence

How being capable and useful hid what was missing.

You learned how to be capable early on.

Not because anyone told you it was a virtue, but because life made it clear—sometimes quietly, sometimes painfully—that needing too much wasn't safe. So you adapted. You paid attention. You figured things out. You became useful.

You learned how to handle things on your own. How not to ask for much. How to make yourself smaller when that was required, and bigger when that was expected.

From the outside, it looked like independence.

You handled things. You solved problems. You carried responsibility with a steadiness people admired. You were the one others leaned on. The one who didn't fall apart.

And honestly—you really did have it together. Your life worked. You moved forward. You built things. You made decisions. You survived. You even succeeded.

But underneath all that competence was something quieter.
Harder to name.

A loneliness that didn't look like loneliness.

Because you weren't alone in the obvious ways. You had relationships. You showed up. You contributed. You were surrounded by people.

And still, there was a subtle absence that never quite went away—
a feeling that no one was fully with you in the places where it mattered most.

Not abandoned.
Not rejected.
Just... alone inside your own experience.

This kind of loneliness doesn't make a scene. It doesn't cry out. It doesn't demand attention. It hides inside strength. It sounds like "I've got this." Like, "I don't really need anyone."

And after a while, you believe it.
You start to confuse how you adapted with who you are.

Not everyone adapted by becoming capable.

Some became agreeable. Or invisible. Or endlessly available.

Some learned to soften, to entertain, to disappear. The strategies were different, but the experience underneath was the same—learning how to stay intact without being met.

What began as a smart way to survive slowly became a way of being. You didn't just do things alone—you started to believe you were alone. Or worse, that being alone was proof of your maturity. Your resilience. Your worth.

You told yourself things like:
I'm independent.
I don't rely on anyone.
I can handle whatever comes my way.

And none of that was wrong.
It just wasn't the whole story.

Because independence, when you choose it, feels spacious.

When you learn it out of necessity, it often feels tight—
even if you can't explain why.

There's a particular kind of exhaustion that comes from being the one who holds everything together. From being the listener. The organizer. The steady one.

You get so good at carrying life that no one thinks to carry you. Eventually, neither do you.

This loneliness doesn't come from a lack of love.
It comes from not being met.

From never really resting into the experience of being accompanied—by someone else or even by yourself. From learning early on that closeness required vigilance. That safety depended on your ability to track, adapt, and endure.

So you stayed alert.
You stayed capable.
You stayed upright.

And the cost of that posture added up quietly over time.

Because while your life kept moving forward, something inside you stayed braced.

Waiting. Holding.
Listening for the moment
it might finally be safe to let go.

At the time, none of this felt tragic. It felt normal. Even admirable. The world tends to reward people who don't need much, who don't slow things down, who don't ask for care.

So you kept going.

You built a life that worked. You became competent, effective, accomplished. You learned how to function beautifully.

And still—if you're honest—there was a quiet ache underneath it all. A sense that something essential had been bypassed. Not missing in a dramatic way, just absent at the foundation.

Like living in a well-built house without realizing there's no warmth in the walls.

This isn't about blaming the past or minimizing the strength it took to survive. That strength was real. It was necessary. You earned it.

But it was survival.

And survival—no matter how polished it becomes—is not the same as belonging. Not with others. And not with yourself.

What you called independence was really you learning how to get by in a world where support wasn't always available. You became your own steady place because you had to.

Over time, that necessity started to feel like identity. And that's where this story begins to loosen.

Because the loyal body remembers—

what the mind learned to live without.

2. Becoming the Container

Why you learned to hold everyone else—people, systems, situations—before you ever held yourself.

Before you ever really knew what it felt like to be supported, you became someone other people could lean on.

You didn't decide to be the strong one. It happened the way these things usually do—quietly, slowly—because it worked.

Somewhere early on, you noticed that things went better when you were paying attention. When you caught the need before it was spoken. When you stayed steady so everything else could stay intact. So that's what you did.

You learned how to hold space long before you learned how to rest inside one.

At first, this looked like competence. You could read a room. You could feel when something was about to go sideways and adjust before anyone noticed.

You knew how to keep things running—people calm, systems moving, emotions from spilling everywhere.

You became dependable. Capable. Useful.

And usefulness started to matter a lot. If you could carry enough—manage enough, understand enough—you could belong. Or at least, you wouldn't be left.

So you learned to contain.

You held the unspoken grief in the room. The anger no one knew what to do with. Fragile egos. Unfinished conversations. The emotional weather that moved through other people and settled in your body.

You learned how to be the steady one, even when nothing inside you felt steady at all. You became the container because no one else was.

Later, people gave it good names.

Leadership.
Sensitivity.
Emotional intelligence.
Strength.

You were trusted—with projects, with people, with responsibility. When something mattered, when it needed care or continuity, you were the one they came to.

You could hold people while they figured themselves out.
You could hold systems together long enough for others to succeed inside them.

From the outside, it looked like mastery.
From the inside, it felt like weight.

Because what no one really saw—not even you, at first—was how much effort this holding required.

Always being a little ahead of the moment.
Scanning for what might be needed next.

Rarely fully inside your own experience, because part of you was always keeping things from tipping.

You weren't resting.
You were bracing.

And the better you got at holding everything, the less likely it seemed that anyone would ever hold you. Not because they didn't care—but because you didn't look like you needed it.

That's the quiet paradox of becoming the container: the stronger you appear, the easier it is for your own needs to disappear. Even from yourself.

You didn't really learn how to receive.
There wasn't much to receive from.
You learned how to give.

Giving was safer.
Giving kept you included.
Giving made you necessary.

And necessity can feel a lot like love—until it doesn't.

Eventually, the body starts to notice the cost. A tiredness that
doesn't lift. A sense that no matter how much you do,
something essential is missing.

What's missing isn't appreciation. Or recognition.

It's being held without having to earn it.
Being held without organizing the space first.
Being held without managing the outcome.

Becoming the container was never a flaw.
It was a smart survival strategy.

It kept you alive. It kept things together. It helped you grow in
places where support was inconsistent or conditional.

But what saves us early on can quietly limit us later.

The container was never meant to be permanent.
At some point, the part of you that learned to carry everything
begins to ask a new question, not in words, but in sensation:

What would it feel like if I didn't have to do this alone?

And when that question appears,

something has already shifted.

Because holding—

is not the same as belonging.

3. Hope as a Survival Strategy

How waiting for love can become its own form of abandonment.

Hope showed up early for you. Not the shiny kind people put on greeting cards. The tougher kind. The kind that keeps going when there isn't much to go on.

Hope was how you stayed upright.
How you made sense of silence.
How you explained absence without letting it break you.

You didn't just have hope. You used it.

When no one was really tuned into you, hope stepped in.
When answers didn't come, hope said they would.
When love felt inconsistent, hope told you it was still real—just delayed, distracted, misunderstood, coming later.

Hope became how you stayed loyal to situations that weren't really listening back.

At first, it felt like strength. Like maturity. Like generosity. You believed that if you stayed open long enough—if you didn't harden, if you kept the door unlocked—love would eventually recognize you.

And sometimes it did—Just enough.

What you didn't notice at first was what hope quietly replaced.

Listening.

Not listening to other people—listening to yourself.
You stopped listening to the small, honest signals that said:

This doesn't feel mutual.
I'm the only one holding this together.
I'm waiting again.
Something in me is tired.

Hope softened signals into something easier to live with:

Just give it time.
They'll come around.
This will make sense later.
Love takes patience.

So you waited.

Waiting started to feel normal.
Waiting felt active, even noble.
Waiting meant you didn't have to name what was missing.

But waiting has a cost.

You waited for conversations that never happened.
You waited for clarity that never came.
You waited for love to deepen instead of noticing
it stayed just out of reach.

You waited for others to choose you—
while slowly un-choosing yourself.

Here's the quiet truth most people don't say out loud:

Waiting for love can become its own form of abandonment. Not
because love never comes, but because you leave yourself while
you wait.

You stop checking in with your body.
You override your instincts.
You put your needs on pause.
You stay emotionally on hold.

Hope points you toward the future.
Listening asks you to stay here.

Listening would have asked harder questions:

What's actually happening right now?
How does this feel in my body?
Am I being met—or imagining being met?
If nothing changed, could I stay?

Hope didn't want answers.
Hope wanted endurance.

And this matters—

Hope was never the enemy.

Hope saved you when there was no other way through. It kept your heart from collapsing. It helped you believe in goodness even when you weren't receiving it.

But survival strategies aren't meant to be permanent homes.

There comes a moment—quiet, easy to miss—when hope stops feeling like expansion and starts feeling like strain. When the body knows before the mind admits it:

This is costing me.

That moment isn't failure.

It's graduation.

It's when listening starts to matter more than waiting. Listening doesn't ask you to give up love. It asks you to stop postponing yourself.

This isn't about losing hope.

It's about letting hope step down from the job of keeping you safe.

Because safety doesn't come from waiting anymore.

It comes from presence.

4. Chasing Connection

When Your Life Revolves Around Someone Else.

There is a way a life can begin to turn around another person without ever being named that way. It does not always look dramatic. It may not even look dependent.

Sometimes it looks like love.
Sometimes it looks like loyalty.
Sometimes it looks like hope.
Sometimes it simply looks like caring very, very much.

But underneath it, your inner world has begun to organize itself around someone else's presence—

someone else's moods,
someone else's attention,
someone else's availability,
someone else's return.

Their shore becomes the place you keep facing.

You may still be living your life on the outside. Still working. Still functioning. Still appearing capable. Still doing what needs to be done.

But inwardly, something in you is angled toward them.

You are listening. Watching. Measuring. Interpreting. Waiting.

Part of you is with them even when they are not with you. And because this can feel so normal, it often goes unnamed.

This overlaps with what some people call codependency, but it is not quite the same.

Codependency is often about over-functioning for another person. This is about over-orienting to them. It is what happens when your inner world begins to revolve around someone else.

Especially if, at some point in your life, you had to organize around someone unpredictable, powerful, absent, intimidating, or dangerous.

Especially if paying close attention to someone else once helped you stay connected, stay steady, or stay safe.

Especially if it has been this way for a long time.

Patterns like this do not come from nowhere. They arise because, at some point, they served you.

Orienting outward helped you read the room.

Helped you anticipate.
Helped you adjust.
Helped you stay near what mattered.
Helped you manage what felt uncertain.

It may not serve you now in the same way. But there was a time when it made sense. Especially if you are—

Used to love feeling like vigilance.
Used to closeness feeling like attention.
Used to caring meaning that a part of you is always turned toward the other person, checking, hoping, tracking, staying ready.

When your life revolves around someone else, it is not always obvious at first. It may simply feel like they matter. But over time, certain things begin to happen.

Your mood becomes too affected by their mood. Your peace becomes too affected by their distance. Your day changes shape around—

whether they call,
whether they answer,
whether they reach,
whether they return.

Their silence takes up too much space.
Their inconsistency echoes too loudly.

Their attention feels nourishing,
and the absence of it feels larger than it should.

Without deciding to, you begin organizing around contact. You think about when to reach out.

Whether to wait.
Whether to say more.
Whether to say less.
Whether you have done too much.
Whether you have not done enough.

You become aware of the thread between you almost all the time. And because they are not always here, longing begins to grow. Not just because you want them, but because part of you has begun to organize around them.

So when they turn away, go quiet, live elsewhere, love inconsistently, or simply fail to meet you in the same place, the emptiness inside the bond begins to magnify.

Then the chasing can begin. You become—

The one who calls.
The one who reaches.
The one who plans.
The one who keeps the thread alive.
The one who carries the emotional labor of connection.

And often, you do not even realize you are doing it. You only know that something in you feels pulled. Restless. Preoccupied. Unsettled.

You only know that you are having trouble coming back to yourself.

This is one of the hardest parts to see.

Because on the surface, it can still look like love. It can still look like devotion. It can still look like chemistry, or tenderness, or deep feeling.

But beneath that, something else is happening. Your inner world is no longer fully centered in your own life. Some part of you is living in response. Watching the weather over there. Waiting for movement over there. Trying to feel settled based on what is happening over there.

And when this has been part of your life for a long time, it can feel ordinary. It can feel like this is simply what caring does.

But there comes a moment when you begin to notice the cost. Not all at once. Not dramatically. Just enough to see it.

Enough to notice how much energy goes outward.

Enough to notice how often you are turned toward the other shore.

Enough to notice how much of the bond depends on your movement.

Enough to notice that your own life is here, but part of you is still circling somewhere else.

That recognition matters.

Not because it fixes anything yet.
Not because it tells you what to do.
Not because the longing disappears the moment you see it.

But because something unnamed has now been named. You begin to see that this is—

Not just love.
Not just desire.
Not just caring.

It is a way of organizing your life around someone else.

And once you see that—

you cannot entirely unsee it.

5. The Day My Solar Plexus Knocked

Where the body spoke first.

Nothing dramatic happened that day.

No unraveling. No confrontation. No visible turning point. If you had seen me from the outside, you would have thought it was an ordinary moment, folded into an ordinary day.

But something inside me was no longer optional.

It didn't arrive as a thought.
It didn't come as fear or insight.
It didn't ask to be interpreted.

It knocked.

It was a sensation—clear and unmistakable, located just beneath my rib cage on the inside. A sharp, focused ache—only enough to get my attention. Not panic. Not overwhelm. More like something that asked me to listen.

And I knew this place.

Before the knock, there were the songs.

Not crafted songs.
Not revised songs.
Not sitting in a room-with-two-other-songwriters songs.

Dictation songs.

They had begun arriving without effort, without doubt, without the usual negotiation between instinct and intelligence.

They came from a very specific place in my body: the center midline, starting just beneath my sternum and extending downward toward my belly button.

Not metaphorically—physically. I could feel them pour out of that vertical channel, as if something had opened and decided it was finally safe to speak.

These were the truest songs I had ever written about my life.

Unedited.
Undiplomatic.
Unconcerned with outcome.

I didn't go looking for them.
They came looking for me.

I could no more stop writing them than stop breathing.

So when a new sensation appeared—just beyond that center line, under my left rib cage—I recognized it immediately. Not as something foreign, but as the same source extending itself. The same insistence, now without words.

I tried, briefly, to turn it into a question.
But it wasn't offering one.

The sensation didn't point me toward an answer. It pulled me closer to myself, like a quiet insistence: listen here.

And I did.

When I stayed with it, memory began to communicate. Not as panic. Not as overwhelm.

The past didn't rush in or demand resolution. It spoke because there was finally a place steady enough to receive it.

For most of my life, everything important had arrived as a story.

I explained my way through discomfort.
I made sense of absence.
I stayed upright by narrating myself into alignment with the facts.

But this didn't need explaining.

This was the body claiming authority—not through force, but through proximity. Drawing me inward. Holding me close enough that nothing had to be defended or justified.

The insistence didn't escalate.
It didn't fade.
It simply remained—steady, faithful, impossible to override.

Something in me had come online.

Not an idea.
Not a role.
Not a decision.

A place.

And from that day forward, when something pulled me close like that—when the body said listen here—I knew it wasn't asking for agreement.

It was asking for presence.

And presence, I had learned—

was no longer optional.

6. The Language Beneath Words

How ache, pressure and tenderness became trustworthy messengers.

Long before you had language for what was happening, your body already knew. Not dramatically. Not with alarms. More like a quiet noticing.

A tightening here.
A pulling back.
A leaning forward.

Before you could say, "This doesn't feel right," something in you had already shifted.

You learned early how to listen to other people's words—tone, mood, timing. You became fluent in the emotional weather of rooms. But no one taught you how to listen to yourself.

So you learned a different language. The one beneath words. It doesn't speak in sentences. It speaks in sensation.

In the hollow under your ribs.
In the warmth across your chest.
In the ache at your waist.
In the way your breath shortens.
In the way your shoulders rise.
In the way your stomach turns before your mind catches up.

This language is honest.

It doesn't negotiate.
It doesn't justify.
It doesn't explain.

It simply says:

Something is off.
Something is safe.

Something is too much.
Something is right.

You didn't lose this language. You learned to override it. To explain it away. To be reasonable. To be accommodating.

You learned to trust coherence in other people's stories more than coherence in your own body. So when your body spoke, you translated it into politeness.

When it tightened, you smiled.
When it withdrew, you leaned in.
When it went quiet, you got louder.
When it felt heavy, you carried more.

Not because you were wrong,
but because belonging seemed to require it.

There is a particular loneliness here.
Not the loneliness of being unseen by others,
but the loneliness of not being witnessed by yourself.

You are present. Capable. Engaged.

And underneath, a part of you is still waiting for translation. This is where anxiety often lives. Not as fear, but as unspoken information. Your body holds data your words haven't learned to carry.

The flutter.
The nausea.
The pressure.
The heat.
The ache.

These are not malfunctions.
They are messages.

The body is not being dramatic.
It is being precise.

It is saying:

This doesn't match.
This isn't mutual.
This is costing you.
This is too much.
This is safe.
This is nourishing.

And it says it before your mind is willing to hear.

Learning this language is not about vigilance. It is about attunement.

Not fixing sensation, but respecting it.
Not interpreting every feeling, but allowing it
to exist without being overridden.

This is what belonging begins to sound like:

a body allowed to speak,
a mind that listens,
a self that no longer has to shout through symptoms.

You don't have to be fluent overnight.
You only have to become curious.

What changed just now?
What tightened?
What softened?
What pulled away?
What leaned in?

This is not therapy language.
It is human language.
The language you spoke before you learned to explain yourself.

And once you begin to listen, something fundamental shifts. You
stop abandoning yourself in small, invisible ways.

Because your body has been telling the truth—

the whole time.

7. The Body as Witness

When the body remembers what the mind protected.

At first, I didn't know what was happening. Nothing dramatic announced itself. No revelation. No collapse. No insight with a headline. What changed was quieter than that—and stranger.

My body began interrupting me.

Not with emotion.
Not with panic.
With sensation.

Clear. Local. Specific.

A place beneath my ribs seemed to tap from the inside and say, listen here.

For most of my life, I believed clarity came from thinking harder. If something didn't make sense, I assumed I hadn't analyzed it enough yet—circling questions, refining interpretations, polishing explanations—convinced that if I just thought clearly enough, truth would eventually appear.

My body had never been invited into that process. So when it began to speak, I didn't recognize the language.

The sensation didn't match anything I knew how to name. It wasn't anxiety. It wasn't fear. It wasn't emotional in the way I understood emotion. It felt more like an ache—small, contained, focused. Insistent without urgency. Often centered in my solar plexus, sometimes elsewhere.

It didn't escalate.
It didn't spiral.
It didn't demand action.

It just stayed.

At first, I treated it the way I treated most discomfort—by moving away from it. I tried naming it. Interpreting it. Explaining it. I tried outrunning it with productivity. I tried understanding my way past it.

None of that worked.

What I didn't know how to do was remain still inside an uncomfortable sensation without trying to resolve it.

But something about this ache felt different.

It wasn't chaotic.
It didn't shout.
It didn't rush me.

It felt grounded. Real. Like a firm pressure against my side saying, this matters.

Stay.

So I stayed.
Not with the story.
With the sensation.

And when I stayed—when I didn't rush to fix it or explain it—something unexpected happened.

Truths surfaced. Not as memories I could narrate. Not as scenes or images. They surfaced as recognitions. Old understandings I had lived by without ever questioning. Internal agreements made long before I had language for choice. Ways I learned to orient myself toward safety, connection, acceptability.

The ache wasn't the problem.
It was the location.

It was where **unfinished body memory** lived—

Truth that had never been fully seen, felt, or completed.
Truth my mind had protected me from knowing too soon.
Truth my body had been carrying quietly, faithfully, all along.

The body wasn't asking me to do anything.
It was asking me to see.

This was new.

I had always assumed discomfort meant something needed to be fixed. Or avoided. Or transcended.

But this sensation wasn't asking for relief.
It was asking for presence.

Stay.
Don't leave.
Don't override.

Just stay.

And as I did, grief began to move. Not dramatic grief. Not collapsing grief. The kind that comes when something true is finally witnessed.

When the watchful body no longer has to hold an unfinished truth alone. When what was once endured in isolation is now met—fully, consciously, kindly.

Nothing was being repaired.
Something was being completed.

The ache softened—not because it disappeared, but because it had been heard. Because I was finally here with what my body had been trying to show me.

This is where belonging arrived.
Not as acceptance from the outside.
Not as safety granted by someone else.

Belonging arrived as presence.
As being fully inside myself.
As no longer abandoning my own signal.
As staying where my body had been pointing all along.

I began to understand that belonging was never something I was meant to earn. It was something I was meant to feel.

And my body—patient, specific, unwavering—had been waiting a very long time for me to arrive.

Once this happened, there was no going back. I could still override myself. I could still leave. But now I could feel the cost immediately.

The body kept receipts.

What surprised me most was that
this awareness didn't make life smaller.

It made it quieter.

Decisions required less effort—
not because they were easier,
but because they were clearer.

My body had already voted.

8. Learning to Stay

Presence not endurance, became the way leaving stopped.

There was no grand moment when I decided to stay.

No declaration.
No promise under a dramatic sky.
No ceremony.

Staying happened the way breathing does—one moment at a time, unnoticed—until one day I realized I was still here.

For most of my life, staying had been conditional. I stayed if I was needed, useful, I wanted enough, chosen enough, tolerated enough. And when those conditions wavered, my body already knew how to leave—emotionally, energetically, sometimes physically—long before my mind caught up.

Leaving was efficient.
Leaving was protective.
Leaving was familiar.

What I didn't know how to do was stay without earning the right to exist.

After my body spoke—after the ache had been witnessed—it didn't ask me to fix anything. It asked a simpler, more confronting question:

Can you stay with this?

Stay with the feeling.
Stay with the not-knowing.
Stay with yourself when there's no audience and no outcome.

At first, staying felt like exposure. Like standing without armor. Like removing the scaffolding that had always held me upright.

My nervous system (the place inside that registers calm or alarm) didn't trust it. Old strategies watched closely, waiting for proof that this was unsafe.

But the body is patient.

It didn't rush me or punish me for flinching. Sensation rose, crested, and fell. Nothing catastrophic followed. No abandonment arrived. No collapse occurred.

Something else did—relief.

Not the loud kind. Not the triumphant kind. The quiet relief of realizing that presence itself could be enough. That staying didn't require explanation. That I didn't have to leave myself just because something felt tender.

This is where belonging began to change.

I began to understand that belonging had structure. It was not made all at once, and it did not arrive from the outside fully formed. It was built in the repeated moments I did not leave myself. Built each time I stayed in my body. Built each time I remained inside the truth of what I was living. What I had once called belonging was slowly becoming structure.

It was no longer something I reached for outside myself—not a role, a room, a relationship, or a future version of me who finally had it together.

Belonging became a felt sense. A steadiness beneath my sternum. A softening where vigilance had once lived.

I began to recognize the difference between being alone and being abandoned. Solitude no longer signaled danger. Silence no longer meant erasure. Rest no longer needed justification.

And staying didn't make me smaller.
It made me more precise.

I stopped chasing the sugar high of activation and began choosing what settled me.

I listened more carefully—to my breath, my pace, the subtle signals that said this fits or this costs too much. I trusted those signals, even when they contradicted old habits or familiar chemistry.

Staying became an act of discernment.

Some people could stay with me.
Some couldn't.
Some chapters closed without drama—only clarity.

There was grief in that, but no panic. No scrambling. No self-betrayal to keep something alive that was already complete.

The ones who stayed were not always the loudest or the longest-known. They were the ones whose presence didn't require me to brace. The ones my body recognized before my mind did. The ones who didn't need me to perform my worth.

And then there was the most important staying of all.

I stayed with the part of me that learned to disappear.
I stayed with the part that survived by becoming competent.
I stayed with the woman who built entire worlds while quietly wondering if she belonged in any of them.

I didn't rescue her.
I didn't rewrite her.
I simply stayed.

This isn't the end of the work. Life still moves. Sensation still changes. Old reflexes still knock from time to time.

But now, when they do, I recognize the sound.

It is no longer a call to leave.

It is a call to notice—

who is here with me now.

9. Who's with Me Today?

Meeting the three-year-old, the seventeen-year-old, and the woman who survived them both.

When I ask, *"Who's with me today?"* Now, the answer is no longer abstract. I know exactly who is.

I didn't learn this all at once. It unfolded slowly, over time in a way I could take in.

The three-year-old is holding on for her life—not metaphorically, not dramatically, but literally. Her entire system is organized around staying alive inside a relationship that was broken and never repaired.

She carries her father through the day the way a child carries a fragile object she believes might disappear if she sets it down. Every movement is careful. Every feeling is a risk. If she lets go, the connection might die. And if the connection dies, she might die too.

She was not allowed to leave her bed. Not physically, perhaps—but emotionally. She learned that movement risked rupture. That reaching could make things worse.

So she swirls.

When she shows up in my body now, she doesn't speak in sentences because she's three. She *shows* me. Images. Sensations. Circular motion. A sense of falling inward with no bottom. A drain that never quite empties, never quite fills—just pulls.

She is not being dramatic. She Is precise.

Her pain isn't loud—it's total and feels endless. It doesn't ask to be solved. It asks to be seen without being rushed toward resolution.

For most of my life, I didn't understand her. I thought she was fear. Or neediness. Or overwhelm. I tried to override her with competence, optimism, self-reliance. I tried to think my way past her.

But she isn't a thought.

She is a **body memory** that never got to finish what it started. And now—finally—I don't ask her to explain herself. I just stay where she is. I listen.

The seventeen-year-old arrives differently.

She is motion. Intelligence. Adaptation. She learned early how to move where the three-year-old could not. If the child had to stay still, the teenager learned how to scan, anticipate, charm, perform, excel. She learned how to become necessary instead of needy.

She carried the hope that connection could be earned.

She is the one who learned how to survive without repair by becoming impressive. By being useful. By being extraordinary. She didn't abandon the three-year-old—she protected her the only way she knew how: by making sure the world stayed interested.

She worked hard.
Too hard.
And I let her.

For years, she drove my choices, my relationships, my endurance. She mistook intensity for intimacy because intensity at least felt alive. She believed urgency was the price of belonging.

Listening to my body taught me something essential:
the seventeen-year-old isn't reckless—she's loyal.

But she's tired.

Now, when she shows up, I let her know she's no longer responsible for keeping the whole world turning. I let her feel what it's like to stand down without disappearing.

And then there is me. I'm learning to listen to parts of myself that once couldn't be heard.

Not the narrator.
Not the fixer.
Not the one who finally figured it out.

The woman who can stay.

I am the one who can sit at the edge of the drain without falling in.
The one who can hold the image without making it into a story.
The one who knows that repair doesn't come from urgency—it
comes from presence over time.

I don't try to rescue the three-year-old anymore. I don't try to
"heal" her in a moment. I don't make promises I can't keep.

I just show up. Again. And again. And again.
I let the body tell me when she's here.
I let the images come.
I let the swirl be what it is.

And something extraordinary happens—not quickly, not
dramatically, but truthfully.

These days, she doesn't have to hold on so tightly because she
knows I'm not leaving.

Sometimes, all three of us are together.

The child holding the memory.
The teenager holding the strategy.
The woman holding the space.

I am no longer confused by their presence.
I am the one who can say without denial, without fixing:

I see you.
I'm here for you.
You don't have to disappear.

That is what the faithful body—

had been trying to teach me all along.

10. We All Like Each Other Here

When no one needs to be fixed or sent away.

For most of my life, I thought inner peace meant control.

Getting the loud parts to quiet down.
The needy parts to behave.
The scared parts to stop embarrassing me.
The hopeful parts to wait more patiently.

I believed wholeness came from editing myself into something acceptable.

What I didn't realize was how crowded it was inside me—not because anything was wrong, but because so many parts of me had been carrying pain without ever being met.

They weren't enemies.
They weren't flaws.
They were hurting.

And I had spent years trying to fix them instead of caring for them.

The shift didn't begin with insight.
It began with a different question.

Not, What's wrong with me?
Not, Who needs to change?
But simply: Who is hurting?

That question changed the tone of everything.
Because pain doesn't need discipline.
Pain needs attention.

When I stopped trying to fix myself and started listening for hurt, something softened immediately.

Not gradually.
Not with effort.
Immediately.

The anxious part didn't need logic—it needed kindness.
The watchful part didn't need dismantled—it needed relief.
The hopeful part didn't need correction—it needed safety.

Even the parts I had judged most harshly—too much, too sensitive, too needy—responded the moment they realized I wasn't here to exile them.

And something surprised me.

I didn't have to work at loving these parts of me. Once I could see that every part of me was trying to protect something tender, love arrived easily. Naturally. Effortlessly.

As the internal threat lifted, the space inside me changed. Not dramatically, but unmistakably. It wasn't a phrase in my mind. It was a feeling.

We all liked each other here.
And it felt like a family reunion.

For so long, there had been walls. Closed doors. Avoided hallways. Not because separation was wanted, but because no one knew it was safe to come back together.

And then, suddenly, it was.

It felt like looking into each other's eyes and knowing: We've been through a great storm. We survived it separately. And now we were finally together.

There was relief in that recognition. A quiet awe.

Nothing needed to be sorted out or explained. No one had to justify their presence. There was just this shared understanding:

We're here.
We made it.
And no one is being sent away.

The system inside me didn't calm down because everything agreed. It calmed down because nothing was under threat.

When no one inside you is afraid of being judged or exiled, the noise softens on its own.

I didn't become simpler. I became kinder.

And that kindness created space—space where I could finally feel at ease inside myself.

Not as a project.
Not as a performance.
Not as something under constant review.

But as a place I could live.

From here, relationships began to change—not because I learned better skills, but because I stopped abandoning myself. I no longer needed someone else to love the parts of me I had already learned to cherish.

And only then did I understand
something I had never been taught:

Before we can truly be accompanied by another—

we have to be accompanied by ourselves from the inside.

11. Being Accompanied

When the body no longer feels alone.

For most of my life, companionship meant proximity. Someone nearby. Someone responding. Someone staying with me at least for a while.

I mistook presence for accompaniment. I thought if there was a body in the room, a voice on the line, a shared project or promise, then I wasn't alone. But I was. I was just not solitary.

There's a difference.

Solitude is being by yourself.
Loneliness is being unaccompanied "inside".

I didn't understand that distinction until companionship arrived—not slowly, not quietly, but all at once—inside grief.

It came in the listening to tears. In receiving truth from my child and teenage parts in pain. In moments of recognition when compassion moved faster than fear—arms around each other, holding without fixing, witnessing without leaving.

Once my body had shown me the truth, and that truth was held in love, something in me knew immediately: I am not alone in here anymore.

An internal reordering began.

What followed felt at times like ache, movement, release, or reorganization. The body does not only carry pain. It also carries the adaptations pain required. And when that pain is finally met with truth, safety, and staying, the body may begin to let go of those old configurations.

That was when the reorganization sensation appeared.

It moved through familiar places in my body that had once carried fear, vigilance, or holding—as if something interrupted long ago was being restored to contact, and my body was coming back into a truer relationship with itself.

Something that had been out of balance for a long time was returning to alignment. It was painful, but less so than before, and it did not last long. The pain felt different now—less like alarm, more like passage.

Those same regions, once restored, began to register something different:

orientation.
completion.
a settling.

From there, a sturdiness followed—not dramatic, not fragile. Just solid. In the days that came after, I walked around accompanied from the inside, as if my body and I were finally on the same side of the conversation.

What took more time wasn't internal companionship.

It was learning how the world landed on me from this new internal configuration.

Out in ordinary life—in conversations, exchanges, everyday moments—my body began weighing in clearly. Signals that once lived at the edge of awareness were now present. Not loud. Not urgent. But unmistakable.

A quiet "heads up—this matters."
A subtle "receive this."
A grounded sense of importance arriving without explanation.

My body wasn't bracing or withdrawing. It was orienting. Letting me know how something was landing, in real time, without commentary or charge.

My body no longer whispered. It simply let me know.

This changed how I understood companionship.

Being accompanied is not something another person gives you. It's not a feeling created by chemistry, reassurance, or consistency. It's a condition of being "with yourself"—without exile, without performance, without leaving in order to belong.

Before this, I had relationships that looked connected from the outside. Productive. Intimate. Even loving.

But internally, I was still performing companionship rather than experiencing it. I was with people while being apart from myself.

That arrangement creates a specific kind of ache—one that doesn't resolve when someone holds your hand or says the right thing. Because the body knows when it is still alone, even in company.

And the body is precise.

When internal accompaniment arrived, something unexpected happened. My hunger for external reassurance softened. Not disappeared—but softened.

I stopped needing someone else to be the container for my experience, because I had become one.

This didn't make me self-sufficient in the polished, independent sense. It made me available.

Available to listen.
Available to feel.
Available to discern who could actually meet me here.

Because people who are internally accompanied are rare.

Most of us were trained to override ourselves in order to belong. To be agreeable. Useful. Palatable. Strong.

And we learned early that staying connected to others often required leaving parts of ourselves behind.

So when someone arrives who is "with themselves", it can feel unfamiliar—sometimes even unsettling.

There's no grasping. No collapse. No performance asking to be met with rescue or acknowledgment.

There is just presence.

And presence doesn't chase.
Presence doesn't merge.
Presence doesn't negotiate its own existence.

This isn't a story about closing off.
It's a story about opening selectively.

Because when you are accompanied from the inside, you don't need to attach in order to feel held.

You can feel the difference between someone who is present and someone who is simply nearby. Between connection that steadies and connection that subtly drains.

Mutuality begins to reveal itself—not as chemistry or compatibility, but as a shared capacity to stay, to be with each other in the moment.

And from here—

closeness was no longer automatic.

12. Nobody Has to Be So Alone

The quiet revolution of inner presence.

After accompaniment, something settles.

Not the relief of being saved.
Not the high of being understood.

Something steadier. A sense that there is someone here now—with you, inside you—who isn't leaving. Being accompanied taught what presence feels like when it's real.

Not performative.
Not reassuring.
Not trying to fix the moment.

Just here.

And once that became familiar internally, something surprising happened. The ache of aloneness changed shape. It didn't disappear. But it stopped being dangerous.

For most of my life, aloneness had meant exposure. No buffer between me and the world. No witness. No soft place to land.

So I kept myself busy being needed.
Useful. Engaged. Entangled.

Not because I loved connection,
but because I feared its absence.

What I didn't understand then was that loneliness wasn't about the lack of people. It was about the absence of internal company.

I could be surrounded and still alone.
Admired and still alone.
Partnered and still alone.

Because no one inside me was actually with me.
That's the part we rarely name.

Loneliness can be internal long before it's external.
Abandonment doesn't always come from others leaving— it comes
from not being met inside.

When accompaniment became real, that equation changed.

The three-year-old wasn't alone anymore.
The seventeen-year-old didn't have to stand guard alone.
And I wasn't the only adult trying to hold everything together.

There was presence now. Steady. Unafraid. Reliable.

And with that, something softened in how I related to other people.
I stopped asking them—without realizing it—to save me from
myself. I stopped leaning forward so hard, hoping someone would
catch what I couldn't yet hold.

Because now, someone was holding it.

This is the quiet revolution no one teaches.

When you are internally accompanied, you don't grip relationships
the same way.

You don't chase resonance.
You don't panic at distance.
You don't collapse when someone can't meet you.

You feel disappointment—but you don't disappear inside it.

Aloneness becomes a state, not a sentence.
Solitude stops feeling like exile.
It starts to feel like space.

And that's when connection becomes more honest.

Because you're no longer asking it to repair your nervous system.
You're asking it to meet you.

Presence changes the terms.

Nobody has to be so alone.
Not because others will always show up,
but because it's possible to become someone who stays.

Someone who doesn't rush the feeling away.
Someone who doesn't abandon the ache.
Someone who can sit beside what hurts without trying to make it mean something else.

The room may still be quiet.
But the quiet is no longer empty.

Something is here with you.

Something that knows how to speak

without words.

13. Silence Is a Language

How the body taught you what your heart had always known.

A quiet, almost unremarkable moment comes when you realize that nothing is asking you to respond.

No problem to solve.
No mood to manage.
No story to fix before it hardens into consequence.

At first, this silence can feel unnerving.

After a lifetime of listening for danger, for disappointment, for what might go wrong, the absence of signal feels like loss. The nervous system scans. The mind offers theories. Surely something must be missing. But nothing is missing.

What's present is silence—not as emptiness, but as information.

For years, your body tried to speak in ways you didn't yet understand. It tightened. It pressed. It lit up in certain rooms and went dull in others. It leaned forward with urgency or pulled back with a quiet, immovable no.

You learned to override it.
To explain it away.
To keep going.

You thought you were being practical. Generous. Mature. But your body never stopped noticing.

Silence, you eventually learned, was one of its clearest languages. It spoke when words failed—when conversations circled but never landed, when apologies were offered but never embodied, when affection arrived with conditions attached. Your body noticed the gaps between words, the pauses that didn't invite rest but required vigilance.

It noticed when you were bracing while smiling. When you were performing agreement instead of experiencing safety. When you were staying because leaving felt harder than enduring.

Your heart had always known this. But the heart speaks softly. And the body, when ignored long enough, learns to speak in ways that cannot be argued with.

There are two kinds of silence.

The first is the silence you endure.

Silence after you speak truth and nothing comes back.
Silence where curiosity should have been.
Silence that asks you to doubt yourself.

This silence feels heavy. Contracting. Your solar plexus presses inward, as if folding into less space. Your breath shortens. Your energy thins. This silence requires work. It demands interpretation. It makes you reach.

The second kind of silence arrives later.

It comes after you stop chasing clarity from places that can't offer it. After you let conversations end without extracting meaning. After you allow distance without filling it with explanation.

This silence feels different. Your body softens. Your breath deepens on its own. There is nothing to prepare for.

This silence doesn't need to be solved. It is spacious. Neutral. Kind.

You begin to notice that when something is right—right enough, right for now—there is very little noise inside you. No rush to define it. No urgency to secure it.

Your body rests into quiet when it is safe.

And when it isn't, the quiet disappears—not as alarm, but as effort. As vigilance. As strain.

This was the lesson your body had been teaching all along:

Silence that costs you your center is not peace.
Silence that gives you your center back is truth.

You no longer need to ask,
"What does this mean?"
You only need to notice:
What does my body do when nothing is happening?
Does it settle—or does it brace?

Your heart had always known the difference.
Your body simply made it undeniable.

And in that knowing, something else becomes possible.

You stop confusing absence with safety.
You stop equating quiet with connection.
You learn that real belonging does not require constant translation.

The truest signals are often the quietest.

Silence is not the absence of language.
It is the body speaking without interference.

And once you learn how to listen, you realize—

you had understood it all along.

14. Being Held from the Inside

When the body starts to learn it's not alone.

There came a moment when strength stopped feeling like something I had to generate.

For most of my life, strength was an action. A posture. A tightening.

It lived in my shoulders, my jaw, my spine held just a little too straight. Strength meant staying upright no matter what. Keeping the system running. Not falling apart.

And then—quietly, without ceremony—that definition dissolved.

I didn't decide to stop being strong.
I didn't rest my way into it.
I didn't earn it.

It arrived as a sensation.
A holding that did not come from muscles.
A steadiness that did not require vigilance.
A support that wasn't braced or prepared for impact.

It felt like something underneath me finally revealed itself.

Not the ground.
Not another person.
Not God.

Me.

But not the me I had been managing.

This was an internal architecture I had never been taught to feel.
For years, my body had been doing containment alone—

holding emotions with nowhere safe to land,
holding decisions without enough information,
holding relationships together with one-sided effort,
holding myself upright when no one else was.

Strength had been a survival response.
A necessary one. A heroic one.

But survival-strength always costs something.

It pulls energy upward.
It tightens the core.
It keeps the system alert even in quiet rooms.

And then one day, my body stopped asking me to do that.

Not because the world was suddenly safe.
Not because life had become gentle.
But because I had become present.

The holding shifted inward.

Instead of pushing against life—I felt supported from beneath it.
Instead of bracing, I felt buoyed.
Instead of scanning, I felt accompanied.

It was subtle.
Almost easy to miss.

A softening behind the sternum.
A fullness where effort used to live.

A sense of "I'm here with you" that didn't come from thought.

This wasn't relief. Relief passes. It wasn't confidence. Confidence
still performs. This was being held by my own nervous system.

The child noticed first.
She didn't ask, Is this allowed?
She simply stopped clenching.

The teenager noticed next.
She didn't need to posture or prove.
She felt less alone inside herself.

And then the adult—the one who had been running everything—
finally exhaled.

I didn't become weaker.
I became less effortful.

The strength didn't leave.
It changed quality.

It stopped being muscular and became structural.
Stopped being reactive and became steady.
Stopped needing to try so hard.

This is what no one tells you about finding your way back to
yourself: At some point, you don't feel fixed.

You feel held.

Not held by answers.
Not held by certainty.
Not held by belief.

Held by presence.
Held by the body trusting it no longer has to do this alone—because
you are finally here.

Strength didn't disappear.
It retired from overwork.

What replaced it wasn't softness in the way we're taught to fear.

It was solidity without strain.
Stability without tension.
Support without demand.

Being held from the inside didn't make me passive.

It made me available.

Available to respond instead of brace.
Available to choose instead of endure.
Available to rest without collapse.

This is the strength that doesn't announce itself.

It doesn't tighten.
It doesn't prepare.
It doesn't prove.

It simply is. And once you feel it—even briefly—you know
something unmistakable:

You were never meant to hold yourself together alone.
You were meant to arrive inside yourself—and be met.

The more you feel yourself held,
the less you search for proof outside you.

And what you once called safety

begins to change shape it

begins to feel like home.

15. Home Is Not a Place

When the body stops searching.

For most of your life, home felt like something ahead of you.

A future room.
A relationship that would finally settle your body.
A version of yourself who would arrive once you got it right.

You kept moving—not always geographically, but internally.
Adjusting. Improving.

Becoming more acceptable.
More useful.
More worthy of staying.

Home, you believed, was conditional.
It would come after the work was done.

But something quiet and irreversible happened along the way.

You stopped searching.
Not because you gave up—
but because the signal pulling you forward went silent.

The reaching softened. The scanning ended. The part of you that was always listening for footsteps finally sat down.

And that's when you noticed it. You were already here.

Not in a house.
Not in a relationship.
Not inside a solved life.

But inside yourself—with nothing braced, nothing held back, nothing waiting to be earned.

Home, it turns out, was never a destination.
It was a body that no longer needed to leave.

You feel it now in small moments.

In how your breath doesn't rush ahead of you.
In how decisions no longer require self-erasure.
In how loneliness doesn't feel like danger—only information.

Home is waking up without rehearsing who you need to be.
Resting without guilt. Letting joy arrive without waiting for the
other shoe to drop.

Home is the absence of performance, acting like you think you're
supposed to be.

For a long time, you thought belonging meant being chosen. But
belonging is what happens when nothing inside you is trying to
escape.

You don't disappear when someone else enters the room.
You don't shrink to keep peace.
You don't override yourself to preserve connection.

You stay. And staying no longer feels like endurance. It feels like
inhabiting.

There is grief here.

For the years you spent believing home was elsewhere.
For the versions of you who kept walking, hoping the next door
would open.

But there is no bitterness in this grief. Only tenderness.

Because those versions did exactly what they had to do to bring you
here—to where seeking could finally stop.

You didn't fail to find home sooner.
Home didn't exist yet.

It required your body to trust itself.
It required safety to be learned from the inside out.
It required you to stop mistaking effort for aliveness.

Arrival wasn't dramatic.

It didn't announce itself.
It felt like relief without a story.

Like sitting down after a long walk and realizing you don't need to stand back up.

Home is not a place you protect.
It is a place that protects you.

And now, wherever you go—into rooms, relationships, work, love—you bring that with you.

Not as armor.
Not as certainty.
But as presence.

You are no longer searching for home.
You are living from it.

And that changes what effort means.

When home lives inside you, relationships stop being rescue missions. They become encounters—and you begin to realize:

Some relationships come to join you.

Some come to mirror you.

And some come to wake you up.

16. The Soul Contracts That Wake Us Up

Why some relationships arrive to reveal truth, not to stay.

Some relationships are not meant to last.

Not because they failed.
Not because anyone did something wrong.
But because their purpose was never permanence.

They arrive like a knock on the nervous system.
Sudden. Specific. Impossible to ignore.

At first, they feel like home. Or recognition. Or relief. Something inside says, "Finally! This is what I have been longing for."

But what's actually happening is more precise than romance, friendship, or destiny. Something dormant is being activated. These relationships don't come to soothe you.

They come to wake you up.

I used to believe that if a connection was intense, it must be meant to last. That depth implied duration. That resonance meant compatibility. Nope!

My body taught me something different.

Some connections arrive not to walk beside you—but to turn you toward yourself. They are mirrors, not destinations. They show you what you have been missing. They illuminate the place inside you that has been waiting—sometimes for decades—to be seen.

And once that seeing happens, once the recognition lands, the relationship no longer has a job. The mission is over.

The body knows this before the mind does.
There is often a moment—quiet, unmistakable—when sensation shifts.

What once felt expansive now feels tight.
What once energized now flattens.
What once felt like possibility now feels like pressure.

Not because the person changed.
But because the lesson has landed.
The contract has been fulfilled.

A soul contract is not a promise to stay.

It is an agreement to reveal.
To reveal where you abandon yourself.
To reveal where you mistake intensity for intimacy.
To reveal where you are still waiting to be chosen instead of
choosing yourself.

These relationships often arrive when you are ready—but not yet
practiced—in truth. They show you your patterns in high resolution.
Their presence is an accelerant.

And because they feel so alive, so charged, it's easy to confuse the
awakening with the person. But the awakening was never about
them.

They were the door.

This is where unnecessary suffering begins. We try to make the door
into a house. We cling. We negotiate. We contort ourselves to keep
the connection alive long after the body has said, enough!

But the body doesn't speak in ultimatums. It speaks in sensation.

And when you've learned its language, you can hear the difference
between love and activation.
Between nourishment and familiar ache.
Between a relationship that supports your becoming—and the one
that only introduced it.

What happens from here depends on what happens to the nature
of the bond.

Letting go of a soul contract can feel like grief without betrayal. There is no villain. No dramatic ending. Just the quiet realization that staying would require you to betray yourself.

This is the ache of releasing something because it no longer fits. The grief of no longer needing what once cracked you open.

And here is the miracle:

When you stop trying to make these relationships last,
they become holy.

You can thank them without resenting them.
Honor them without chasing them.
Release them without erasing their importance.

They were not mistakes.
They were initiations.

And something else becomes possible. When you no longer confuse awakening with attachment, you become available for relationships that don't need to shake you to get your attention.

Relationships arrive after your truth has settled.
Relationships that feel calm—steady.
Unremarkable to the nervous system—
and extraordinary to the soul.

Not every soul contract ends in goodbye. Sometimes what dissolves is only the version of the relationship that carried the lesson. The urgency fades. The roles loosen.

And what remains is quieter, simpler—a bond that no longer asks anything of you, a bond that finally knows how to rest.

Some relationships wake you up.
Others walk with you once you're awake.

Learning the difference is not a failure of love—it is refinement.

And the body—faithful, patient, precise—will always tell you

which is which. If you are willing to listen.

17. Mutuality

Reciprocity isn't an idea—it's a felt sense.

For most of my life, connection felt like a quiet calculation.
How much of me could I bring before it tipped the balance?
How much did I need to give to stay welcome?

I didn't think of it that way at the time. I would have said I was generous. Loyal. Committed.

I would've said I showed up. And I did. But underneath all that showing up was a truth my body knew long before I did: I was relating from effort, not from rest.

I learned early that connection required attentiveness—reading the room, anticipating needs, smoothing edges before they cut.

I became skilled at it.

Skilled enough that it passed for intimacy.
Skilled enough that I didn't notice what was missing.

What was missing was mutuality.

Not equality.
Not sameness.
Mutuality is subtler than that.

It's the felt sense that you are not alone in the exchange. That the weight doesn't live on one side. That your body doesn't have to brace to remain connected.

I didn't know to look for this. I had learned to measure connection by endurance—by how long I could stay present without asking for too much. By how well I could adapt.

Mutuality, when it finally appeared,
didn't arrive with fireworks.
It arrived with relief.

I noticed it not as a thought, but as a physical shift. My shoulders didn't lift when the other person spoke. My breath didn't shorten. I didn't feel the need to manage the exchange.

There was space.

I could pause without consequence. Speak without rehearsing. Listen without disappearing.

Nothing dramatic happened. That was the point.

Mutuality didn't ask me to perform closeness. It didn't ask me to earn safety. It met me where I was.

That's when I understood:

Mutuality isn't an idea. It's an experience.

You don't think your way into it.
You feel your way there.

And once you've felt it, your body remembers.

I learned to recognize its absence not as a concept, but as a pattern. When I find myself taking most of the actions, I step back—

From being the one who always reaches out.
From keeping the thread from dropping.
From noticing the distance and closing it.
From making sure the connection doesn't fade.

None of these are wrong.

They are gestures of attention, tenderness, hope. But when they mostly belong to one person, something quiet has shifted. The connection isn't moving on its own anymore. It's being carried.

Stepping back isn't withdrawal. It isn't punishment. It's information.

It returns you to your own place in the exchange and lets you see what's actually there when you stop holding it together.

Mutuality doesn't make every relationship symmetrical. Life isn't built that way. But it does recalibrate what is sustainable.

What no longer works isn't difference or conflict. It's effort without return. Presence without being met.

When mutuality is absent, your body tells you—often before your mind is ready to listen. And when it's present, your body doesn't need to say much at all.

It rests.

That rest became my compass.

Not toward certainty.
Not toward perfection.
But toward relationships where I could remain intact.

Where depth didn't require vigilance.
Where closeness didn't depend on
just me holding it in place.

I could stay open without bracing.
I could care deeply without disappearing.
I didn't have to do it alone anymore.

And from here—

closeness was no longer automatic.

18. Choosing Who Gets Close

Letting non-mutual relationships float without making them villains.

There is a quiet moment that arrives after enough listening—a moment when you realize you are no longer trying to convince anyone to stay.

You are no longer earning closeness, explaining your worth, or translating yourself into something easier to hold.

Something in you has shifted from pursuit to discernment.

This isn't about ending relationships.
It's about choosing proximity.

For most of your life, closeness felt negotiable.

You learned to stay available, adaptable, generous.
You learned how to widen yourself so others wouldn't have to.

When connection faltered, you assumed it was your job to bridge the gap—to offer more clarity, more patience, more understanding.

But your body has learned something your mind couldn't access before: Closeness that doesn't let you rest is not intimacy.

As your inner regulation grew, so did your capacity to feel difference—not difference as judgment, but as information.

Some people settled your system. Others stirred it. Some relationships moved toward you naturally, without pressure. Others required effort, explanation, or self-erasure to maintain.

And for the first time—

You didn't turn that noticing into a story about fault.
You didn't make anyone wrong.
You simply noticed what was mutual.

Mutuality doesn't announce itself loudly. It feels like ease without collapse. Presence without performance. Communication that doesn't require decoding.

It lives in the absence of bracing.

And when it's missing, something else becomes clear:
You don't need to villainize a relationship to let it float.

This is where old patterns often try to reassert themselves.

The part of you that learned love through endurance may want a reason—someone to blame, a narrative to justify distance.

But the work you've done allows a softer truth:
Not all relationships are meant to be close.
Not all distance is rejection.

Some connections were vital at one stage of your life.
Some taught you how to survive.
Some reflected who you were becoming, even if they couldn't walk with you the whole way.

Gratitude and boundary can coexist.

Letting a relationship float doesn't mean cutting it off or hardening your heart. It means releasing the expectation of reciprocity where it doesn't naturally exist. It means allowing connection to find its correct altitude.

When you stop forcing closeness,
something remarkable happens.

Your system relaxes.

You no longer scan for responses.
You no longer wait for attunement that doesn't come.
You no longer shrink or expand to maintain access.

Instead, you become selective—
not from fear, but from steadiness.

Choosing who gets close is not a test of loyalty or love.

It is an act of self-respect.

And as you choose proximity based on mutual regulation rather than emotional intensity, your relationships reorganize themselves.

The ones that can meet you step forward.
The ones that cannot drift—

without drama,
without accusation,
without loss of dignity.

This is adulthood at the nervous-system level.
You no longer ask, "Why don't they choose me?"
You are asking, "How does my body feel here?"

And that question—quiet, honest, embodied—will not lead you astray.

19. The Afterglow

How your body lets you know you do not leave yourself.

Afterglow is not the moment itself.

It's what happens after something has occurred—
when the room empties,
the song ends,
the conversation concludes,
the car pulls out of the parking lot—and your body does not rush to
collapse back into loneliness or vigilance.

Afterglow is what stays.

We often judge meaningful experiences by their peak—the high of a
great night, a strong show, a room that lifted. You want to do it
again as soon as possible, hoping to capture that feeling.

But peaks are intensity. And intensity passes.

Not all warmth that follows an experience is afterglow.
Some warmth comes from intensity.
Some warmth comes from shared connection.

Afterglow is different.

It is the warmth that follows coherence.
It does not replace connection.
It confirms that you felt safe enough to be yourself.

Afterglow is quieter.

It doesn't announce itself.
It doesn't demand anything.
It simply remains.

Afterglow is physical.

It arrives as warmth through the center of the body.
A spreading ease.
A sense of inner company.

Nothing is pulling you forward.
Nothing is chasing you from behind.

You don't need to replay the moment.
You don't need to secure reassurance or plan what comes next.

It is what the body feels when you stayed.

For most of my life, meaningful moments were followed by a drop.
Even when something had gone well, I would begin adjusting,
preparing, measuring how it landed.

The warmth never had a chance to remain.
Not because the moment was wrong—
but because I had already left myself inside it.

Afterglow feels different.

The moment ends and there is

No collapse.
No tightening.
No inner scramble.
No sudden need to interpret what just happened.

There's warmth instead—
a steady alignment through the center of the body.

Not excited.
Not relieved.
Aligned.

I began to notice that afterglow had nothing to do with how
impressive the moment was.

It appeared
when I had not guarded.
When I had not performed.
When I had not angled toward being received a certain way.
When I let the experience be what it was and stayed inside it.

When the focus stays on what others are thinking—
the moment collapses afterward.

When the focus stays with the body—
The moment doesn't collapse.

That's the difference.

Afterglow does not take root where approval is being
silently negotiated.

Afterglow is feedback.

The body softly registering:
You did not leave.
You were here.

Afterglow is a signal that something important has changed—
you belong to you now.

It feels like being supported from the inside.
As though my own actions formed
something solid enough
to stand on.

Not because the outcome was good.
Not because someone approved.
But because I stayed with myself while it was happening.

That staying has weight.

20. Once We Learn How to Stay

Why this isn't enlightenment—it's availability.

For a long time, I thought the goal was transcendence.

To rise above reaction. To quiet the ache. To outgrow the places in me that still flinched, still reached, still hoped.

I imagined some future version of myself—lighter, calmer, less vulnerable—who would no longer be moved so easily by connection or loss. Someone who had finally figured it out.

But that isn't what happened.
What arrived was not elevation.
It was contact.

Staying did not lift me out of my humanness. It dropped me into it. Learning how to stay doesn't make life less intense. It makes it more honest.

The sensations don't disappear.
They become legible, easier to understand.
The waves still come; you just stop running from the shoreline.

Before, when something stirred inside me—warmth, tightening, grief, longing—I treated it like a problem to solve or a message to decode so I could move on.

Insight became a form of exit. Understanding was how I left my body politely.

Staying asks something different—It asks you not to leave when the moment opens. Not to rush sensation into meaning. Not to trade presence for clarity.

Availability is not a spiritual achievement.

It is a relational one—first with yourself.

It's the capacity to remain with what is happening now
without turning it into something to manage.

Without promising yourself it will resolve soon.
Without making it useful.

This is where the shift actually occurs.

Not when the pain ends.
Not when the joy peaks.
But when you stop bracing for either.

Staying means you don't disappear from your own experience just because it's unfamiliar or uncomfortable.

You don't abandon the warmth when it spreads.
You don't shut down the ache when it lingers.
You don't outsource your attention to what it "should" mean.
You let the moment have you.

At first, this feels like vulnerability without armor. There is no banner to wave, no identity to claim—just the quiet, unnerving intimacy of being here for what is real.

But something else begins to organize from the inside.

When you stay, your body learns it doesn't have to escalate to be heard. Sensation softens into signal. Emotion stops shouting. The internal room grows steadier—not because you're in control, but because no part of you is being sent away.

This is how belonging becomes structural.

Each time you stay, something in you becomes more reliable. More able to remain. More able to feel without fleeing, and to know without abandoning yourself. What once felt fleeting begins to take shape from the inside.

This is not awakening as spectacle.
It's awakening as reliability.

You become someone your own experience can trust.

Over time, this changes how connection works.

You no longer seek intensity to feel alive, because aliveness is already present. You don't confuse activation with intimacy. You can feel closeness without losing your footing—and distance without collapsing into interpretation.

Staying does not make you immune to longing—
It makes longing safer to feel.

And because you are no longer trying to escape yourself—You stop asking relationships to rescue you from your own interior. You arrive with availability instead of need. Curiosity instead of demand.

This is the quiet miracle:

Nothing has been fixed—
and nothing needs to be.

You are here.
With yourself.

And that turns out to be enough to hold

whatever comes next.

21. This Is How I Stay

I carry my own light into the room.

I didn't cross a finish line.
I just started showing up for myself.
Not in dramatic moments—in ordinary ones.

I stay by meeting myself at predictable points in the day.
When I wake up.
When I sit down to eat.
Before I go to sleep.

I don't wait for something to be wrong. I simply return.

The question I ask is uncomplicated:
"Is there anything in me that wants to be noticed right now?"

Sometimes something speaks.
Sometimes nothing does.

I've learned that quiet is not avoidance.
Quiet is what safety sounds like.

Staying isn't about intensity.
It's about allegiance.

It's about returning often enough that nothing inside me
has to raise its voice to be heard.

There are small moments every day when something in me is
invited to leave—to rush, to appease, to perform, to disappear into
usefulness or explanation.

Staying means I notice. Not to correct myself, but to orient—Am I
about to leave myself to make this easier?

Sometimes staying looks like slowing my body down before my
mind catches up. Letting a sensation finish its sentence. Waiting
long enough to feel what yes or no actually does inside me.

Sometimes it means—

Choosing rest when urgency demands productivity.
Choosing truth when politeness would keep things smooth.
Choosing fewer words when over-explaining would feel safer.

Staying is not endless examination. It is completion.

When something needs action, I take it.
When something needs reassurance, I offer it.
And when something has been understood, I let it settle.
There is no need to reopen what already feels finished.

It isn't heroic. It's curious.

When I feel uncomfortable in my body or my mind starts to swirl,
I know I need to get close to myself.

It looks like carrying a small light down a hallway inside myself. I
don't know what I'll find. But I walk anyway.

My inner "hoper" still whispers, "Maybe this time."
My inner "bargainer" still suggests, "What if we adjust just a little?"
My inner "longer" still wonders, "When will they come back?"

They didn't disappear when I grew.
They quieted enough to be met.

Instead of silencing them,
I listen and put my arm around them.
"Of course you feel that way."

Staying does not mean eliminating reflexes or shaming longing.
It means following sensation to its root and reminding my body: we
are not standing in line anymore awaiting discipline.

What's beautiful is—I do not have to control the world to feel
steady in it.

I let ambiguity be ambiguous.
I let longing be longing.
I let people be who they are.

And I remain.

The bigger part of me is not afraid.
The younger part of me is allowed to emote.

Somewhere between the two, a quiet confidence rises:
I can meet the world on the world's terms.

There are days when staying feels warm.
There are days when it feels ordinary.
And there are days when it feels like work.

But something has shifted.

I am no longer negotiating my presence.
I am no longer earning my own company.

Staying is not about holding tight. It's about not leaving.

This is how inner belonging takes shape:
someone inside you keeps coming back.

And once there is someone inside you who keeps choosing you—
morning, midday, night—something quietly radical becomes true:

You are never alone in your own life again.

That is how I stay—

I carry the light.

22. Approval Is Not Belonging

When the body feels safe enough to stand.

If we are agreeable, we are welcomed.
If we answer quickly and correctly, we are not attacked.
If we soften ourselves just enough, we remain included.

Approval brings relief.
Relief can feel like safety.

Over time, the two become fused.

And when safety and approval are fused, the body learns to shrink.

The breath lifts high in the chest.
The sternum tightens.
Words arrive before thought.

We monitor tone. We adjust mid-sentence.
We position ourselves slightly below whoever holds power.

Not because we are weak. Because we are protecting connection.

Shrinking is not politeness. It is protection.

You may still speak.
You may still function.
But part of you is scanning.

Approval-seeking splits the self.

Part of you is expressing.
Part of you is negotiating.
Part of you is asking, "Will I still be safe if I say this?"

Afterward, there is churn instead of warmth.
Replay instead of steadiness.
Collapse instead of afterglow.

The problem is not wanting to be liked.
The problem is making being liked
the condition for being yourself.

When approval outranks alignment, shrinking begins. And shrinking feels safer in the moment.

It reduces friction.
It lowers risk.
It keeps connection intact—temporarily.

But the body knows the cost.

Belonging is different.
Belonging does not depend on someone else's reaction.
Belonging is remaining intact while you speak.

It is allowing pause.
It is saying, "I need to think about that."
It is clarifying terms without apology.
It is disagreeing without collapsing.

Approval may or may not follow.
Belonging remains either way.

Unlinking safety from approval changes everything.
When safety no longer depends on being liked, the breath deepens.

Our inner "stander-upper"—the part that knows your true size—is finally given permission to stand up.

Not aggressively.
Not defensively.
Simply upright.

The question shifts from
"Will they like me?" to
"Can I remain intact while I speak?"

Those are not the same page.
The first is about protection.
The second is about coherence.

Coherence creates warmth.
Warmth creates afterglow.
Afterglow becomes support.

It is possible to be kind and firm.
Warm and clear.
Connected and equal.

Approval can feel like oxygen.
Approval can feel like being safe.
Approval can feel necessary.

But belonging is structural.

When safety and approval are no longer fused—

we can stay without shrinking.

23. Overwork Is Not Devotion

How hustle tried to replace safety.

You learned to work so you wouldn't disappear.

Not explicitly. Not ceremonially. But in the small, daily ways that taught you what mattered—the relief that spread across a room when you said yes, the way problems softened when you arrived early, stayed late, filled the gap, figured it out.

Being needed kept you visible. Carrying more kept you included.

Over time, work became more than effort.

It became posture. It became protection. Movement kept things from falling apart. Productivity kept you visible. As long as you were doing, producing, responding, nothing could ask you for what you didn't have.

Hustle wasn't ambition. It was insurance.

Overwork doesn't begin as devotion to a dream.

It begins as devotion to safety.

You learned—without language—that stillness was risky. Waiting invited disappointment. If you stayed indispensable, you stayed included.

And for a long time, it worked. Your life functioned. Systems ran. People relied on you. You built things—good things, meaningful things. From the outside, it looked like commitment. Like passion. Like grlt.

Inside, something quieter was forming.

Your body learned that love arrived through effort.
That belonging came through contribution.
That rest had to be earned—and even then, briefly.

Overwork became a language.

One that said: I'm here. I matter. I won't disappear.

Beneath that was a deeper fear—quieter, but more binding.
That if you stopped, you would fade. Not dramatically. Not all at
once. Just—slip out of view.

As if the project itself were the tether holding you in place.
As if completion were proof of existence.

So you kept going.

Not because the work needed you—but because you needed the
work to confirm you were still here.

This is how overwork hides. It dresses itself as responsibility while
quietly carrying the fear of erasure.

For a long time, work did what it was asked to do. It kept you here.
You worked so you wouldn't disappear.

Sometimes you worked because you loved something so much you
could not bear for it to move slowly. And sometimes it started as
true financial circumstances, but striving didn't stop when the need
was no longer severe.

Urgency can wear two masks:
fear and devotion.

But beneath both is the same belief—
If I don't push, it won't happen.
If it doesn't happen, I will fade.

This is how overwork matures. Not through greed. Not through ego.
But through urgency becoming your identity.

And then your body began to tell the truth. Not loudly. Not with
collapse. Just in small refusals.

A fatigue that sleep didn't touch.
A tightening when your calendar filled too quickly.
A subtle dread at the thought of pushing through.
A moment when you felt you couldn't pick your hands up anymore.

You had grown used to a tiredness sleep could not fix. It wasn't physical exhaustion. It was the fatigue of bracing.

This wasn't failure. It was discernment. Something in you had matured enough to know what your mind couldn't yet accept: safety does not come from constant output.

It comes from staying.

And once staying began to build safety and structure inside you, work no longer had to do the job of keeping you here.

This was the real transition.

You were no longer asking effort to do the work of belonging. You were no longer depending on urgency to create the feeling of continuity, value, or place. What hustle had once tried to provide from the outside was now beginning to form within.

You noticed something that contradicted the old story.

The first time you worked without urgency, nothing collapsed. You made decisions calmly. You moved steadily. You completed what mattered.

And your body stayed warm instead of braced.

Things arrived. They did not attach themselves to your nervous system. They landed—and either stayed lightly or rolled off.

That was spaciousness.

No one had ever defined it for you. There was no cultural language for it. Only this—

a body not gripping.
A mind not stacking tasks.

You didn't vanish during pauses. You didn't disappear when things slowed. You were still here—breathing, sensing, present—without performing continuity.

The project wasn't keeping you alive. You were. And when that landed—not as insight, but as lived experience—the urgency loosened.

Work didn't disappear.
It simply changed roles.

Work as expression.
Work as contribution.
Work as choice.

Not as shelter.
Not as proof.
Not as survival.

Just something you do—while living the rest of your life.

Nothing extraordinary happened.

And it was ordinary and miraculous at the same time.

24. Creativity Without Abandonment

There's no performing in belonging.

Creativity asks for presence.
Business asks for outcomes.

For anyone who makes things for a living—or hopes to—
the two become entangled early.

What begins as listening, curiosity, and play
slowly acquires an audience.

Then an evaluation.
Then a scoreboard.

At some point, many creators realize they are no longer only
creating. They are anticipating. Translating. Pre-editing themselves
in the direction of what might be wanted.

Without noticing when it happened, the business side of creativity
took the lead. There is a moment when you realize that some
standards cannot be met because they were never meant to be
universal.

They are written into particular lives.
Particular timing.
Particular networks.
Particular tastes.

Trying to meet them from the outside slowly hollows you out.

This is where many artists become quietly unhappy with their own
work. Not because the work is wrong—but because it has been
placed in service of something that cannot reliably receive it.

A song is no longer a song. It becomes a test.
A painting is no longer an exploration. It becomes an evaluation.
Creation becomes something you do while looking over your
shoulder.

The industry is not the enemy. But it is also not the authority on what is true. Its role is secondary.

It responds after the fact.
It amplifies selectively.
It confuses access with merit and timing with destiny.

When the industry becomes the narrator of the creative act, something essential is lost.

The creator's job is not to predict the market. It is to protect the signal. The act of creation requires a different posture—one willing to make what is true today without guarantees about tomorrow.

This isn't naïveté. It's accurate. Because nothing genuinely alive is made from calculation alone.

There is no marked path for work that comes from the center. Only a lived one. When you create from your own axis, several things change quietly.

You stop using rejection as evidence against yourself.
You stop confusing preference with judgment.
You stop abandoning the present moment in hopes
of securing the future.

The need for approval had been pulling you out of direct experience—out of the moment where the work was actually happening.

When that pressure softens, authenticity is no longer something you achieve. It is what remains when you are present enough not to leave yourself.

The business becomes a conversation—not a verdict.

From here, creation regains its abandon. Not reckless abandon, but grounded abandon. The kind that trusts the work to become itself before asking it to perform.

This is how creativity becomes a way of belonging to yourself.

Even in environments that measure selectively.
Even when outcomes remain uncertain.
Even when recognition arrives unevenly—or not at all.

For a long time, the industry trained sensitive gifted people
to reach upward.

Toward approval.
Toward permission.
Toward proof.

Even when it wasn't desperate, it was depleting. Reaching up keeps
your center elsewhere. It keeps your worth offshore.

It also pulls you out of the moment, which is the only place creation
can actually occur. The more approval leads, the harder it is to stay
with what is true as it is happening.

That's when work begins to lean away from the body. Away from
listening. Away from pleasure.

Creation becomes something you do while scanning the horizon—
waiting for confirmation, hoping the right person will turn their
head. And then—sometimes quietly, sometimes all at once—
something shifts.

You realize you're no longer reaching up.
Or even reaching toward.
You're just reaching out.
From where you already stand.

That is the difference between hunger and appetite.
Between striving and choosing.
Between "someday I'll belong" and "I'm here."

There is an honest recognition that may follow:
If I had that accolade, I would be welcomed everywhere.
Yes. And it's also beside the point now.

Because what arrives in this shift is something the industry can
neither give nor revoke: Satisfaction without collapse. Self-regard
without comparison.

This is where creativity reorganizes itself.
The business no longer narrates the work.
Taste no longer masquerades as truth.
Rejection no longer reads as indictment.

You stop confusing access with worth.
You stop confusing timing with destiny.
You stop asking tomorrow to justify today.

You speak and choose from what feels true inside you—

and let the future take care of itself.

25. Holding Without Hovering

How your energy comes back when you stay.

For many people, life requires reaching out.

You send the email.
Make the call.
Share the work.
Offer the idea.
Extend the invitation.

This isn't occasional. It's daily. Sometimes hourly. Creative, relational, and professional lives all depend on contact.

And yet, for many of us, the reaching out is not the hard part. What comes "after" is. Because once something is sent, a familiar pattern begins to run underneath the surface:

Wait → wonder → manage feelings → decide whether to act.

On the outside, this can look like:
patience, consideration, emotional intelligence, maturity.

On the inside, it is anything but restful.
Waiting becomes hovering.
Wondering becomes monitoring.
Managing feelings becomes pre-emptive emotional labor.

Deciding whether to act becomes an ongoing negotiation about tone, timing, worth, and permission.

Nothing has happened yet—and the body is working overtime.
This is not a flaw. It is a survival pattern.

Many of us learned early that reaching out carried risk. Silence could mean rejection. Delay could mean disinterest. No response could mean something about us.

So we didn't just reach out—we stayed with the outcome.

We tracked it.
We braced for it.
We rehearsed disappointment.
We softened ourselves in advance.
We left ourselves and went to wait somewhere else.

Over time, this hovering became normal.
Exhausting—but normal.

What changes everything is not learning how to reach out less.
It is learning how to release without abandoning yourself.

A simple reorientation makes all the difference:
Send → release → live.

You send the thing—the message, the work, the invitation.
And then you release it.

Release does not mean you don't care.
It means you no longer stay emotionally tethered
to someone else's timeline.

You do not wait inside their silence.
You do not manage imagined feelings.
You do not pre-live outcomes that haven't arrived.

You come back to yourself.
You stay in your own life.

If something comes back, it comes back.
If it doesn't, it doesn't.

Either way, you are still here.

This also changes how you respond when something "does" require
action.

Instead of living inside:
Wait → wonder → manage feelings → decide

The body learns a simpler sequence:
Notice → say → move on.

You notice what is real. You speak it calmly. And you move on without carrying it. No rehearsal. No emotional choreography. No internal permission-seeking. Just reality, named.

This is not harshness. It is clarity. And clarity costs far less energy than hovering ever did.

For many people, the body has been doing heroic work under the surface for years—carrying the invisible weight of unanswered messages, delayed responses, imagined outcomes, and emotional labor no one ever saw.

When recognition arrives, the body doesn't need to push anymore. Energy returns. Movement becomes easier. Reaching out stops costing so much. Creativity no longer requires self-abandonment.

And this is where belonging comes in.

Belonging is not something granted by response, approval, or timing. Belonging is staying centered in your own life while participating fully in the world. It is belonging to yourself without leaving your body waiting somewhere else.

You can send the song, the book, the idea, the invitation.

And then live.

Not because the outcome is guaranteed—
but because you remain at the center of your life.

That is belonging.

That is how creativity becomes spacious instead of costly.

That is how you are no longer alone—

because you never leave yourself

to begin with.

26. When Hope Steps Back

Hope is the tether that keeps longing in place.

For most of my life, hope felt like a virtue.

Hope meant I was loving.
Hope meant I was faithful.
Hope meant I wasn't giving up on people.

I didn't realize hope was also the reason I couldn't see clearly.

Hope has a way of keeping our eyes on who someone "could be" instead of who they are. And as long as we're focused on their potential, we have a hard time seeing what's actually right in front of us.

This isn't denial. It isn't naivety. It's the way we learn to cope when we've had to wait for people to change in order to feel safe.

Hope acts like a soft lens over the eyes.
You are not blind. You are gently blurred.

But hope does more than blur what we see.
Hope keeps longing in place.

When your life has revolved around someone else, longing becomes almost inevitable.

Part of you is turned toward them.
Part of you is waiting there.
Part of you is still organized around what might come from them.

And hope keeps that arrangement alive. Hope says—

Maybe they will come through.
Maybe they will choose me.
Maybe they will love me the way I need.
Maybe then I will finally feel settled.
Maybe then I will be okay.

Longing is the ache.
Hope is the tether.
Longing hurts,
but hope keeps it facing outward.

Hope keeps the other shore positioned as the place where relief,
rescue, love, or completion might still come from.

So the longing does not release simply because it is painful.
It does not release simply because you are tired.
It does not release simply because the relationship is costing you.

As long as hope remains necessary for survival, part of you will keep
turning outward.

I used to think clarity would help me stop hoping.

What I learned is the opposite—I could only see clearly after hope
was no longer needed for survival.

As long as I needed someone to become different
so I could feel safe, hope stayed in place.

And as long as hope stayed in place,
I could not fully see how this relationship
was affecting me.

I could not fully see what it was costing me
to keep my life turned toward the other shore.

It is like trying to understand what alcohol is doing to you while you
are still drinking it.

You cannot assess the impact from inside the influence.
You can only see it once you step out from under it.

When I finally learned how to stay with myself,
stay with my messy, unreasonable want—
something quietly happened.

Hope finally stepped back.

Not because I forced it to.
Not because I argued with it.
Not because I became cynical.
But because I no longer needed it to feel okay.

I was no longer using hope to hold me together.
I was no longer asking hope to promise me a future
through someone else.

And when hope stepped back,
my view changed instantly.

I could see, without drama and
without bitterness,
what was true.

That clarity did not feel painful. It felt calm.
Because it was not a decision.
It was a recognition.

I didn't stop hoping in order to see clearly.
I learned to stay, and hope was no longer required.

And once hope was no longer required—

I could finally see.

27. Longing and the Other Shore

How the body kept connection alive in the absence of certainty.

Longing is one of the most misunderstood emotional states we carry. It's often mistaken for love. Or hope. Or faithfulness.

But underneath, longing is usually something quieter—and more structural—than any of those.

Longing is orientation.

It is the part of us that remains subtly angled toward someone else—their growth, their return, their awakening, their recognition.

Even when the relationship has ended.
Even when contact has stopped.
Even when the story appears complete.

Longing keeps a line open.

Not because anyone asked us to, but because at some point in our lives, staying oriented outward was how we survived.

For many people, longing formed early.

It arose in environments where love was inconsistent, incomplete, or conditional—where staying emotionally linked felt safer than letting go. Hope became steadiness. Waiting became devotion.

And so longing learned to live deep in the body—not always as ache, but as readiness. A background posture of "not yet." A quiet keeping of space.

This is why longing can be difficult to recognize. It does not always feel painful. Sometimes it feels noble. Sometimes it feels patient. Sometimes it feels like love that has not given up. But the cost is subtle and cumulative.

Longing keeps us tethered to someone else's shore. Even as we move forward. Even as we grow. Even as we believe we are free.

Some part of the self remains turned toward what is not here. Some part of the body remains available—to someone else's arrival, someone else's change, someone else's eventual return.

That is what makes longing so powerful. It is not only desire. It is a form of inner positioning. The body keeps a relationship active—

long after mutuality has weakened,
long after the mind has tried to move on,
long after the visible story appears to be over.

This does not mean the love was false. It means the body learned how to keep connection alive in the absence of certainty.

There is tenderness here, especially toward the younger parts of us that learned to keep hoping because hoping felt safer than release. Those parts do not need to be shamed. Longing did not come from weakness. It came from adaptation.

It helped preserve connection.
It helped keep a line open.
It helped us survive the absence of what we needed by continuing to lean toward it.

But longing was never meant to be the place we live.

At some point, the cost begins to show. Energy keeps going outward. Attention keeps traveling elsewhere. Part of the self remains subtly tethered, subtly preoccupied, subtly unfinished.

And because longing can feel so much like love, it often goes unnamed for a very long time.

But longing is not only love. It is a life still angled toward someone else—a body still keeping watch, a heart still leaving space, an inner world still holding a line open. And until that orientation changes, some part of us remains there.

There comes a time—quiet, almost easy to miss—when the tether begins to loosen.

Not because time has healed it, but because you no longer abandon yourself to maintain it.

At first, this may not feel like grief. It may feel more like disorientation. A strange emotional neutrality. The absence of anticipation. A lack of pull.

For many people, this moment is frightening. If longing has always been the engine, what happens when it stops?

What is important to understand is this:
the quiet that follows is not emptiness—

It is unlinking.

The body is recognizing that it no longer needs to stay oriented toward someone else in order to feel alive. The work longing once did—keeping connection alive in the absence of mutuality—has finished.

Longing did its job. It helped you stay open where others could not fully care for you. But it was never meant to become your home. At some point, the body begins asking a different question.

Not, "Will they come back?"
Not, "Will this resolve?"
But: "Do I still need to stay oriented outward in order to be here?"

When the answer changes, longing does not disappear all at once—it retires. And what replaces it is not indifference. It is direction.

Energy begins to reorganize—slowly, quietly—back toward the self. Not in isolation, but in sovereignty.

The tether dissolves.
The shore releases.

What comes next is not always immediately clear. The wind may be absent for a while. But the boat is no longer anchored to someone else's promise.

And sometimes, in that quiet, a recognition arrives: This pattern lived in the body for a very long time. Maybe decades. But the reorganization is underway.

Longing was never a wound that required fixing. It was a strategy that once kept you intact. And now, without force or ceremony, it is finishing its work.

Each time you choose yourself without leaving—each time you stay present rather than reach outward—the body adjusts. It learns it no longer has to keep watch. It no longer has to hold space for someone else's becoming. It is safe to stand where it is.

What unfolds next is not dramatic. It is steady.

Orientation shifts. The center holds. You are with you.

The relationships that once lived in the foreground move gently into the background, where all relationships belong. And belonging is no longer something sought across distance. It is here.

Not because longing was healed—but because it was finally allowed to rest.

You—are the axis your world turns around now.

And yet, this is not the end of longing. Longing does not disappear when we belong to ourselves. It changes ground.

Before belonging, longing often tries to hold us up. It becomes orientation, and hope keeps it tethered as a way to feel less alone in a world where we have not yet learned how to stay with ourselves.

From that place, longing carries too much weight. It tries to be connection and stability at once.

But after belonging to yourself—after hope steps back—longing is no longer asked to do survival work. It becomes what it was always meant to be: a desire for shared presence.

We do not need someone to complete us—We need someone who can occasionally sit beside us while we complete ourselves.

From this ground, longing is no longer frantic or consuming.
It is honest. It is spacious. It is simply the human wish
not to carry life alone all the time.

And there is nothing unhealthy about that.

28. Held at Last

The body keeps the long memory of truth.

There is a moment that arrives
without announcement.

Not as relief,
Not as triumph,
Not as the closing of a chapter—
but as a quiet internal fact:

I am being held.
Not by circumstances lining up.
Not by someone finally staying.
Not by a future version of myself who has it all together.

Held from within.

It arrived as steadiness. A sense that nothing inside me needed to reach outward to stay upright anymore. A sense that I could stand right where I was—inside an ordinary moment—and not brace.

The first time I noticed it clearly, I was not alone.

I was in a community room where music had landed—where voices and listening braided together—and afterward, instead of crashing or dispersing, I felt the room still holding us. Not mystically, but somatically.

The moment didn't vanish when it ended.
It stayed as a settled presence inside my body.

That sensation began to show up elsewhere. I was sitting beside my daughter at a wedding, surrounded by people, receptive, present.

Nothing was wrong.
Nothing was required of me.

And suddenly my middle warmed—slow, spreading, gentle—like something inside me gathering me from side to side, holding my center together.

It wasn't nerves. It wasn't emotion looking for an explanation. It was my body saying:

"We're okay here."
"We don't need to leave."

I didn't analyze it. I just let it be there—a lived confirmation that I could remain present inside connection without scanning, without effort, without disappearance.

These are not peak experiences.
They are settling experiences.

For most of my life, connection had been followed by fallout. Intensity followed by depletion. Closeness followed by cost. Even good moments asked for payment later.

But this was different—Afterward, I was still with myself. Nothing had left the building.

That's when I understood something essential: being held is not about being taken care of. It's about not being abandoned—by yourself—inside your own experiences.

I had spent decades building strength as a substitute for holding. Managing as a stand-in for safety. Functioning as a form of belonging.

But this—this didn't need strength. It needed presence.

Held at last, didn't feel like being wrapped up.
It felt like standing on ground that no longer shifted beneath me.

There was no urgency to name it. No impulse to preserve it.
No fear that it would disappear if I didn't do something right.

When holding comes from within,
it doesn't demand maintenance.
It simply remains.

Something else surprised me.

My inner child isn't facing the world. She's facing me.

Even when I feel her in my chest or solar plexus, the orientation is
unmistakable—face to face. Arms around my neck.
Not braced. Not scanning. Just close.

This matters—

For most of my life, the forward-facing space inside me was
occupied by others—by the people I tracked, waited for, oriented
around. My attention moved outward. My body learned vigilance.
Togetherness, when it existed at all, was something I tried to earn
or manage.

This is different.

When the child part no longer faces outward, she has been relieved
of her post. She is not on watch duty. She trusts that I am here—
that I can face life without her standing guard.

Her job now is simpler, and more profound: relationship.
She looks at me—I look back. This isn't dependency.
It's completion.

One part of me is oriented outward—available to life.
One part is oriented inward—available to love.
Connected, but not fused.

This is what being held feels like from the inside.

Not intensity.
Not collapse.
Not disappearance.

Just closeness without agenda.

I didn't train this posture. My body found the configuration that
finally made sense—where no part has to be exiled, and no part has
to be brave. This is how inner togetherness becomes safe.

Face to face.
Heart to heart.

And slowly, another realization surfaced.
My body has been holding my truth across time.

It carried the hope, held the longing, braced when it had to,
softened when it could, kept sending signals even when I couldn't
listen yet.

The loyal body reminds—not as accusation, not as verdict,
but as a quiet guardian.

It keeps the rhythm of what happened and what healed.
It remembers survival and belonging in the same breath.

It does not rush.
It holds the timeline until we arrive.
There is grief in that recognition.
But there is also relief.

This is not an ending.
It's not a resolution.
It doesn't tidy up the story.

It is a place to stand. A place—Where relationships can come and go
without taking you away from yourself.

Where creativity moves through you without costing your center.
Where joy doesn't require vigilance afterward.
Where hope no longer substitutes for mutuality.

Held at last, is not the absence of pain.
It is the absence of leaving.

Belonging to yourself changes the shape
of every day that follows.
Life is no longer something
to endure, but an experience
you can stay inside.

You are with you
You are in you.
You're smiling.
You belong—to you.

29. If This Finds You Lonely

A letter to the reader who hasn't felt this yet.

If you arrived at this page because something in you feels alone,
I want to tell you—I know this place. Not just loneliness as the
absence of people, but loneliness as the absence of yourself.

The kind that can exist in a full room.
The kind that aches in the center of your chest.
The kind that hides inside a life that looks like it's working.

If you are here, it doesn't mean you failed to arrive.
It means your system learned to survive without being
accompanied—You adapted.

At some point—maybe early, maybe repeatedly—you learned that
staying present with yourself wasn't safe, useful, or rewarded.

So you learned to leave gently. Quietly. Competently.
You learned to be strong without being held.
To be good without being met.

And even while that worked,
something in you still felt the cost of it.

If you haven't felt what I describe in this book—the internal
companionship, the sense of being held from the inside—I want
you to know this isn't something you can force or figure out.

What I didn't understand at the time, was that something was
quietly changing in the way I related to myself.

It didn't start as healing. It started as self-protection.

I listened to my body and let it speak to me because it hurt.
I opened my journal because I didn't trust what I'd do if I didn't.
I wrote because I needed somewhere to put the ache.
I spent time with me because there was no one else in the room.

Just a fireman running straight into the fire carrying a notebook.

There was no grand intention to build a relationship with myself. No declaration. No turning point. Just small acts that were building something inside I had no knowledge of and no words for.

At some point—so quietly I almost missed it—the act of listening to what I felt inside and writing it down stopped feeling like a task and started feeling more like company.

Nothing dramatic happened. No revelation.

Just a subtle softening.
A little less urgency.
A little more space around the ache.

And the answers to my questions about me,
about everything—began to surface.

Looking back, I can see what changed wasn't that I was healed. I was able to gently lay down the patterns that once protected me

once I could see them,
once I could feel them,
once I stopped leaving myself.

It was that simple. Not easy sometimes, but simple.

The Big Book of AA has twelve steps.
This book has one—stay.

When you stop leaving yourself, belonging begins in ways that don't reverse. Something in you recognizes the direction home—
and keeps walking.

The conditions didn't change all at once.
They changed through repetition.
Through listening that didn't demand answers.
Through showing up without shutting down
the heart-wrenching, screaming,
messy longing in me.

And over time, something else happened too.

Before, I listened because there was no one else in the room.
Now I listen and feel someone here in me.

Not a new voice.
Not a perfected self.
Just presence where absence used to be.

My presence.

If you are still waiting for that feeling—please know this:

Your small acts of staying count.
Your pauses count.
Your listening counts.
Your decision not to abandon yourself in one moment—even if you
do in the next—counts.

Inner companionship grows quietly.
Often before you know what to call it.

So if this finds you lonely—let this be enough for now:

You may still be learning how to stay without bracing.
How to rest without disappearing.
How to listen without fixing.

Or you simply may not yet feel,
what staying is doing within you.

These are not small skills.

If like me—you've been to counseling, you may already know this:

What happens in the room matters.
But what you do with yourself in between
matters just as much.

No one can do this part for you.

It takes honesty.
It takes time.
And it takes a willingness to be with yourself
in a way that may not feel natural at first.

Your mind may doubt that any of these actions matter.
But your body is quietly recording every moment you stay.

There were times I crumbled—wondering whether my mind would ever catch up after so many decades spent oriented outward.

What I didn't know at the time was that those small acts were not disappearing. They were gathering into something.

Belonging has structure.
Staying helps build what is missing,
reveal what is hidden,
and restore what fear disrupted.

The more we stay with ourselves—especially in the moments we once would have left—that structure begins to take shape.
Begins to restore what's been lost.

The loyal body does not measure progress in breakthroughs—
It measures safety in repetition.

And over time, those small acts create an internal structure sturdy enough to feel at home inside yourself—a living home where mutuality becomes possible.

It's no mistake you found this book.

Even here.
Even now.

Something in you is already practicing.

You are not alone in feeling alone.

And it will not always be this way.

30. The Container Holds

When your body refuses to let you abandon yourself.

There was a time when a small shift in connection would have taken you under. A glance. A tone. A pause in a text thread.

You would not have villainized the other person.
You had already outgrown that.

But you would have turned the ache inward.
You would have sat with it.
Carried it. Interpreted it. Felt it as loss.

Your body would have tightened and stayed tight. Not because you were weak. But because hope had been tied to survival.

Hope can be beautiful.

But survival-hope grips.

It echos—

Maybe this will secure you.
Maybe this person will steady you.
Maybe this connection will keep you from disappearing.

The mind can move quickly in that direction. Old tapes do not ask permission.

But something new began to happen.

The body moved faster. A pressure in the back. An ache beneath the ribs. A subtle constriction that said, gently but clearly—No. Not this way.

Not punishment. Not panic. Just a flag. And this time—

You did not override it.
You did not suppress it.
You did not follow it into story.
You noticed.

When the container of your own body begins to feel safe—
it does not need to scream.
It whispers. It corrects lightly.
It metabolizes quickly.

The mind may reach for an old pattern. The body answers: We don't
live there anymore.

And because you listen, the sensation passes. The bind releases. The
projection retracts. The thought loses charge. Nothing dramatic
happens. And yet everything has changed.

This is mastery without force.

Not controlling your thoughts.
Not eliminating attachment.
Not hardening against hope.

It is responsiveness.

You feel the old movement begin. You stay.
Your body completes the correction.
The container holds.

And when the container holds—

You do not need another person to stabilize you.
You do not need urgency to feel alive.
You do not need projection to feel connected.
You remain. Warm. Grounded. Here.

When you stop leaving yourself, something unexpected happens.
What once would have lingered for days now dissolves in minutes.
Not because you are detached. Because you are home.

And then, without announcement—

Something else begins to change.

31. The Field of Belonging

Belonging without gravity and the space that holds us.

As I learned to stay with myself, the chronic vigilance my body had carried for years slowly began to fall away. And as it did, something else began to show itself.

What once felt grounded now felt light.

In the lightness, a softer quality of presence appeared—a quiet atmosphere formed when nothing in me was pulling away.

I noticed it first as sensation. Warm. Spacious. Light.

A gentle buoyancy moved through my body, as if gravity had softened without disappearing.

I was still here—still in my life, moving through the ordinary rhythm of an evening—and yet something fundamental had changed. I was not bracing toward anyone, and I was not holding myself back from anyone either.

For much of my life, belonging carried weight. The weight came from a subtle outward orientation. The center of gravity in my world lived somewhere beyond me—in another person's response, warmth or recognition.

I did not know how heavy those lines were until they loosened.

That evening, I rested before an upcoming meeting and felt something unfamiliar: a quiet sense of being supported without effort.

The feeling of being lifted was there.

I carried that atmosphere with me into the meeting—into conversation, into creativity, into silence, into shared moments.

Songs were played. Writers shared their work. A publisher-friend and I sat listening, offering thoughts, weaving conversation. I spoke when ideas came. Generosity flowed easily, not as performance but as overflow. There was no calculation about when to contribute or how much to offer. Nothing needed managing.

The room lingered.

People stayed past the formal ending, not because they had to, but because no one seemingly felt pulled elsewhere. Familiarity felt like homecoming rather than history.

And within it all, I felt what I had first felt on stage at the community room, and subtly in some recent co-writing sessions.

My presence cost me nothing.

Ideas came without searching.
Encouragement flowed without depletion.
Mutuality existed without negotiation.

This is what I came to understand as belonging without gravity.

Belonging that does not depend on securing a place.
Belonging that does not require self-erasure.
Belonging that does not ask us to hold the room together.

Belonging that arises when our own presence becomes the place from which we live. As our inner relationship settles, the outer world becomes easier to meet.

It is belonging that remains when the subtle contracts of longing loosen. It does not remove connection. It transforms the field where connection happens.

We stand alongside rather than reaching toward.
We participate rather than perform.
We contribute without measuring the cost.

In these moments, we are not only experiencing belonging,
we are participating in the Field of Belonging—a field that becomes visible when we stop organizing ourselves around someone else and are organizing around ourselves.

Our nervous systems recognize the safety of the shift.

They begin to co-regulate.

In that field, certain qualities begin to appear:

Conversation becomes spacious.

Ideas arrive without searching.

People feel free to be themselves.

The room itself says, *"Count me in!"*

No one wants to leave.

Silence feels natural.

Time leans back and says, "Take your time."

Mistakes dissolve in the moment.

Simply being there is enough.

Lightness and play return.

I felt this in my body before I ever had words for it.

The sternum that had held subtle bracing for years began to soften,
not dramatically but gently—pliable rather than armored.
Breath moved differently.

The space behind my shoulder blades widened and warmed, as if
effort were redistributing itself without instruction. Nothing felt
exposed. Nothing felt vigilant. There was simply availability.

Later, I picked up my mandolin.

An instructor once told me to wear my instrument rather than hold
it, but only now did I understand what that meant. The leather strap
crossed my shoulder and, for the first time, I could feel it resting
there. My shoulders dropped. Breath moved underneath the wood.
The instrument was no longer something I held—it was
something I wore.

I felt accompanied by it.

Not because the mandolin was alive, but because relationship does
not belong only to living things. Instruments hold memory in their
wood, in the way sound responds to touch, in the quiet

companionship of vibration meeting breath. I played without defense. The music felt like it was in me and all around me.

Who knew belonging is wearable.

Belonging without gravity did not make me float away from life; it allowed me to move through life without the subtle weight of proving I belonged.

When the evening ended, I did not leave energized in the way accomplishment often energizes. I left open. Peaceful. Tired in the gentle way that follows shared experience rather than self-expenditure. I ate. I rested. The buoyancy remained—not as a peak, but as presence.

Belonging without gravity does not announce itself loudly. It does not demand explanation. It often arrives quietly—

Nothing inside needs to strain toward connection.
Nothing inside needs to withdraw.

We are simply here.

This does not mean longing disappears forever
or that bracing never returns.

It means we begin to recognize moments
when neither is organizing our presence.

We taste what connection feels like when urgency is absent.

We discover that participation can be effortless,
that warmth can exist without negotiation,
that creativity can move without the pressure of outcome.

In these moments, Belonging is no longer
something we seek. The room no longer
has to hold us.

We arrive already belonging.

The Field of Belonging itself is never missing.

It surrounds every gathering of human life—quietly present in living rooms, cafés, rehearsal spaces, meeting rooms, and crowded bowling alleys alike.

What changes is not the field but our orientation within it.

When we are vigilant—consciously or unconsciously—our focus narrows. But when even one among us is held on the inside—no longer looking to the room to supply their worth or safety—awareness widens.

The field and all of its characteristics become visible—and available to everyone present. And something subtle begins to happen. The room finds a shared rhythm.

Belonging spreads.

In this widening—belonging becomes something we no longer seek.

Belonging becomes the field from which we live—
sensed in breath, presence, and relationship,
carrying us without weight and
gently inviting the world in.

Belonging without gravity reveals itself
as spacious connection,
effortless contribution,
and presence.

Not a final destination,
but a lived reminder
that we are not alone.

We belong in the gentle space of our own presence.

And from that place,

we meet one another—

without weight.

32. Breaking Up with Urgency

When the body finally smiles.

One day you notice something surprising. The thing that used to make you rush… doesn't.

There is still work to do. Details to finish. Decisions to make. But the familiar pressure isn't there.

Urgency left the building.

What you feel instead is simpler.
You're ready. But you're not bracing.
And that's when you realize something important.

Urgency is no longer needed.

For a long time, urgency felt necessary.
It looked like responsibility.
It looked like devotion to the work.

But beneath it was a constant message:

Something is at stake.
Move faster.
Solve this now.

Sometimes urgency and safety become linked without us realizing it—If I stay ahead of everything, I will be safer.

Urgency becomes a kind of early-warning system.

It scans the future,
pushes forward,
makes sure nothing slips.

Over time it can feel like the only way life works.

And the body takes that very seriously. It holds tension, stays alert, and keeps energy mobilized because somewhere along the way it learned: Relaxing might not be safe.

Urgency narrows the world. The body tightens. Attention contracts. The future begins to feel like something that must be secured before you can relax.

Urgency can help us accomplish things.
It can help us survive difficult seasons.
But eventually something begins to change.

The shift rarely begins in the mind.
It begins in the body.

The familiar pressure simply isn't there. There is still work to do, but nothing feels at stake in the same way. Danger dissolved. Only later does the realization arrive.

You are here—with you.

The equation begins to change.

Instead of: Urgency = safety
The body senses: Belonging = safety

A series of experiences tell the nervous system a new story.

You stayed with yourself.
You felt being held from the inside.
Relationships became more mutual.
The Field of Belonging appeared.

All of these experiences signal to the body that something in the environment has changed. The future no longer needs to be secured before you can breathe.

And when the body realizes this, urgency begins to lose its hold. Something else takes its place. Energy without pressure. Care without strain.

You still want to move forward.
You still feel ready for the next step.

But readiness is different from urgency.
The body knows the difference.

When urgency leaves, attention widens.
Creativity returns. Curiosity returns. Playfulness reappears.

Life is no longer organized around solving something.
It becomes possible to simply live.

To move easily from one thing to the next without pressure.
To care about the work without carrying it like a burden.

Letting go of urgency does not mean letting go of commitment.

The work can still matter deeply.
You can still move forward with devotion and care.

But the future no longer has to be wrestled into place.

The body can rest while the work continues.
The body knows when an old strategy is no longer needed.
It does not argue. It simply stops participating.
The pressure fades. The urgency disappears.

And when the body releases what it no longer needs to carry,
the mind eventually understands. Something inside you has already
moved on. You are free to follow.

And in the spirit of honoring all the ways

we have tried to protect ourselves,

we offer these words of appreciation.

Dearly Beloved,

We gather here today
to celebrate the passing of Urgency.

For many years Urgency served faithfully.
It carried responsibility,
kept watch through difficult seasons,
and pushed us forward
when everything felt at stake.

We thank Urgency
for its years of service.

But its work here is done.

Urgency is survived by
Curiosity,
Playfulness,
Steady Devotion,
and a body
that finally knows it is safe.

May it rest in peace.

33. Turning Point

When the body feels like a trusted friend.

There comes a moment when the storm that has lived inside you for so long finally moves through. Not because you solved it, forced it, or outran it—but because you stayed.

The longing, the confusion, the aching pull toward someone who could not fully meet you—all of it rose, moved through the body, and slowly released its grip.

For a long time it felt as if your body itself was the problem.

It was the place where longing flared,
where hope returned when it shouldn't,
where the old patterns kept lighting up like a live wire.

But one day something quiet and surprising happens.

The body that once carried the pain begins to carry the wisdom.
The same place where the longing once lived becomes the place that says, "I've got you."

This is the part that changes everything.

We didn't reason our way here.
We didn't argue the mind into peace.
We stayed with the body long enough for it to feel safe again.

And when the body settled, the mind followed.

The thoughts that once spun in circles grew quiet—not because they were forced to stop—but because the body no longer needed to sound the alarm.

The turning point doesn't arrive with fireworks. It comes quietly.

You find yourself in the same room with the person who once unsettled you, and something inside simply stays steady.

You can speak, laugh, even share a moment of music or conversation and when it's over—you are still yourself.

The center holds.

That is when you realize the journey was never about eliminating longing or erasing love. It was about discovering the place inside that remains intact—

no matter who is present,
no matter who leaves,
no matter what the heart once hoped for.

From there, life opens again
not as a storm to survive,
but as ground beneath your feet.

The body is no longer something you have to manage or mistrust. It has become a companion.

The path you've walked begins to make sense, and the center you found along the way begins to feel reliable.

And for the first time, belonging doesn't depend on who stays.

It's already here—because you stay.

And you're not going anywhere.

34. A Citizen of Belonging

A map of what's possible when no one leaves themselves.

When the Field of Belonging appears, a new kind of citizen emerges. Belonging stops being a moment—and becomes a place.

There is a country called Belonging.

Some people are born there.

They arrive into bodies that are welcomed, mirrored, protected enough that belonging never fractures. To them, being themselves feels natural. Rest is not dangerous. Listening inward does not require courage. They assume this is how everyone lives, because they have never known otherwise.

And then there are others.

People born into fracture—into inherited fear, instability, silence, violence or vigilance. People whose bodies learned early that staying required adapting. That safety came from paying attention outward. That connection meant overriding inner signals. That belonging lived somewhere else.

Most of us don't know that this has happened.

We only know effort.
We only know striving.
We only know the ache of something unnamed.

So the world rarely talks about it.

Those who have belonging do not know to name it.
Those who lack belonging do not know what to name.

And so we misunderstand one another endlessly—
mistaking inheritance for character,
and survival for choice.

Belonging is not a personality trait.
It is not confidence.
It is not resilience.
It is not optimism or faith or grit.
Belonging is a place you live inside yourself:

Belonging has laws, though they are not written:
You do not abandon yourself.
You do not override yourself.
You do not earn your right to exist.
You do not disappear to stay connected.
You do not ask another to rescue you from yourself—
But they may stand beside you while you stay.

Belonging has boundaries.
You know when to stay.
You know when to leave.
You know when something is not for you.
You know where you end and another begins.

Belonging has structure, built one moment of staying at a time.
You're not standing in a doorway—wondering if you are allowed in.
You're not visiting.
You're not waiting for permission.
Nothing is leaning on you for balance.
Nothing inside it asks you to
contort, brace, or perform just to stay.

Belonging has walls.
Not to shut the world out—but to hold you up.
They contain your presence.
They give you strength to stand.
Stillness begins to gather.
Rooms begin to make sense.
They protect you from the weather of others.
The wind stays outside.
The roof can finally do its job.
The house becomes inhabitable.

Belonging has a door.
A threshold where choices
are made about what gets close.

Belonging has rooms.
Rooms for meeting.
Rooms for living.
Places where love, rest, truth, and mutuality
can enter and take their seats.
And no room is meant for indefinite waiting.

Belonging has shelter.
Its roof says, come here and take cover from the storm.
Its hearth says, I will keep you warm.
Its foundation says, I will not give way beneath you.

Belonging has direction.
The body's compass asks different questions.
Not "What's exciting or impressive about them?"
But "Do I feel steady, calm—more like myself when I'm with them?"

Belonging has safety.
Not the absence of pain,
but the presence of someone inside you
who does not leave when pain arrives.

Belonging has rest.
You do not endlessly scan outward.
You do not work until you're depleted.
You do not rush—but let presence do its quiet work.

The mind searches for belonging.
The body searches for safety.

Safety is built by staying.
And when the body finally feels safe,
belonging begins.

Arrival is not a feeling.
It is a relocation.
I stopped leaving myself.

I did not become better.
I did not become healed.
I did not transcend my past.

I arrived.

I learned to listen and stay.
I learned to trust the voice beneath the sternum—
quiet, steady, unarguable.

I built home where there had once been only effort.

Some people are born home.
Some people build home.

And I have become a citizen of Belonging.

Not because I was chosen—

but because I chose to stay.

All are welcome.

Unlinking

As Not Alone begins to wind down—
I can feel the tenderness of something changing form.

It has been companionship.
It has been delight in seeing the truth arrive.
It has been wonder in the release.
It has been gratitude so strong it brought me to tears.
It has been the long, holy feeling of waving goodbye
to a shore I was once tethered to.
It has been the growing power to be truly me.

This was never only a book.
It was a lived unfolding.
A transformation in real time.

And the book kept finding a way to hold it.

What is happening in me is not finished.
What opened is still opening.

It will live in the next things I write.
It will live in the life I am living now.
But it will never again be the first time.

There is afterglow in that.
And there is ache in that too.

Maybe this is one of the first transitional moments
I have known I could simply stay—

Stay with the feeling.
Hold it gently.
Give it a kiss on the cheek.
Walk it to the car in the driveway.
Wave goodbye as it leaves the house.

And say,

I will still be here for you Not Alone.

I will still be here as you take your next steps.

Acknowledgments

I am grateful to those who listened while the words were still forming, who helped me stay with myself long enough to hear what mattered.

To my daughters: you were the first place these conversations lived. Your lives, your questions, and your courage shaped more of these pages than you know.

To the songwriters and artists I've worked alongside: thank you for your risk-taking and your willingness to bring yourselves fully into the room. You continue to teach me what mutuality looks like in practice.

To the reader—
Thank you for your willingness to stay with this book.
If you recognized yourself in these pages,
if anything in you softened, steadied, or felt less alone,
I'm glad we met here.

To my body—
Thank you for holding what I could not yet feel
and for returning it to me
when I was ready.

An Invitation

While writing this book, I developed a process that helped me stay with myself as feelings and discoveries unfolded.

If you'd like to explore this process yourself, you can download the workbook freely at NancyDeckant.com.

About the Author

Nancy Deckant is an author and songwriter based in Nashville. Her work explores belonging as a lived experience—one shaped not through achievement or approval, but through return to oneself. Her writing asks what becomes possible when we stop reaching outward and learn how to stay, choosing not to leave ourselves when something is uncomfortable, uncertain, or unfinished.

After a lifetime of preparation, Nancy found herself in a brief and intense season where everything she had gone through turned and faced her all at once.

Nights of journaling followed—not as effort, but as refuge. Curled up in bed, writing became a place where truth could emerge, where tears could fall, and where something steady could finally be felt beneath the storms she had lived with for so long. She did not know then that this quiet practice was building structure.

Alongside her work as an author, Nancy has spent decades in the music industry as a professional songwriter and founder of Discover Sooner, a global creative development platform helping songwriters meet music industry professionals and Nashville Cool, a music publishing company.

Her work with songwriters and artists is grounded in listening, relationship, and trust—supporting creativity without asking the self to disappear in the process.

Today, Nancy lives from a place she once didn't know existed— accompanied and at home with herself. This book was written from that arrival.

Other authored works are The Songwriter's Guide to Protecting Your Songs and Collecting Your Money.

More about Nancy's writing, music, art and about belonging can be found at nancydeckant.com.